What is a Story?

Also by Don Cupitt and published by
SCM Press

Christ and the Hiddenness of God
Creation out of Nothing
Crisis of Moral Authority
The Leap of Reason
Life Lines
The Long-Legged Fly
The New Christian Ethics
Only Human
Radicals and the Future of the Church
Taking Leave of God
The World to Come

DON CUPITT

WHAT IS A STORY?

SCM PRESS

British Library Cataloguing in Publication Data

Cupitt, Don
  What is a story?
  I. Title
  230.01

ISBN 0–334–02419–6

First published 1991
by SCM Press Ltd
26–30 Tottenham Road London N1 4BZ

Typeset by J&L Composition Ltd
and printed in Great Britain by
Clays Ltd, St Ives plc

For John

Contents

self-possessed and self-conscious. We are unavoidably caught up in all the uncertainties of interpretation. We find that we ourselves are just as hard to read as other people are. Because we are temporal beings, and therefore immersed in becoming, we are compelled to be liars, dreamers, fantasists, actors, mountebanks and con-artists who live by our wits, borrowing or improvising our many stories as we go along. We are always chatting each other up, selling ourselves, trying to convince each other by spinning our yarns. When we are caught out we have to think fast and invent a story to get out of trouble. An old Army friend of mine was wont to say grimly of one or another of his delinquent soldiers: 'That's his story, and he's stuck with it.'

However, this view of human life as a tissue of fictions, though as I say common enough among dramatists, novelists and other imaginative writers, has always been anathema to the great tradition of Western philosophy that stems from Plato. Philosophy believes in tenseless, non-narrative Reason; it believes in the timeless unity of Truth, the unity of virtue and the unity of the self. Above all, it has believed in transparent and simultaneous rational self-possession. It considers the artists and writers to be seducers and deceivers, and regards their suggestion that fictions may be truer than truth as a frivolous paradox.

Interestingly, although our religion is itself highly narrative, a great body of stories and ritual dramas, it nevertheless chose from the outset to ally itself with the philosophers *against* myth, *against* the theatre, *against* the free play of the imagination and *against* masks, time, ambiguity and play-acting. In order to maintain its distance from pagan religions and its hostility to the theatre and pagan art, Christianity was obliged in some measure to repress its awareness of its own narrative, mythic character. The repression betrays itself in the violence with which religious people still sometimes attack 'immoral' and 'blasphemous' plays, films and novels, and the very sharp hostility with which they have greeted the modern introduction of the word 'myth' into theology. The presumption has usually been that Christian beliefs express straight, unambiguous, non-narrative dogmatic Truth, and the whole tradition has favoured a character-type that is in no way 'double' (i.e., theatrical, ironical or duplicitous).

Like a stick of Blackpool rock, the saint is supposed to be exactly the same all the time and all the way through. The saint has to be just what he or she appears to be, transparent to the point of simplicity, always the straight man in life's comedy double-acts and never the joker. So completely do we take this for granted that we find it very difficult to imagine what would happen to virtue, to personal integrity and to religious belief if we were fully to accept the fictionalist view of the human world and the self.

Nevertheless, it is time for us to start imagining. In the modern age the old objective order of tenseless Reason has disappeared, and there has been a turn to subjectivity. This has created an insatiable demand for stories of selfhood. Since about the time of the Romantic Movement old-style Philosophy and theology have got weaker and weaker. Instead, the fictioneers — artists, writers, personalities, performers and directors — have come to dominate the culture. They invent and market new forms of selfhood, new dreams and new lifestyles. They are mythmakers, who give us new stories to live by. Meanwhile, philosophy itself is reluctantly becoming more ready to admit its own literary and indeed narrative character. A thin line of overtly literary philosophers, most of them anti-systematic thinkers and writers of satires and aphorisms, can indeed now be traced back as far as the late Middle Ages. During the present century figures such as Kierkegaard, Nietzsche and Freud have become highly influential, and the recent explosion of interest in literary theory has affected both philosophy and theology.

It may seem, then, that our agenda is clear. Since antiquity there has been a certain tension both in the culture at large and in religious thought between philosophy and myth, timelessness and time, theory and story, reason and imagination. Now that the culture is less oppressively rationalistic than it was, and now that most people are ready to allow that myths and other fictions can convey profound truths, surely all we need is a really lucid explanation of exactly what stories are and what kind of knowledge they give us? Such an explanation might heal a long-standing rift in the culture, bringing scientific understanding and imaginative creation closer together. It might even provide the basis for a new religious apologetics.

Unfortunately matters are not quite that simple. Paradox is not easily avoided, for any such clear theoretical explanation of the nature of stories would merely perpetuate the old subordination of *muthos* to *logos*. We would in effect be reiterating the old doctrine that myth and art are no more than a colourful disposable packaging in which pure conceptual Truth is wrapped for popular consumption. Such a doctrine effectively explains myth and art away – and therefore does not explain them at all, for it does not leave anything distinctive and important for stories to be except packaging. However, the alternative is equally problematic, for if I were to write a myth about the nature of myth, the concept 'myth' would be presupposing itself in order to explain itself. There is a similar problem about works of art whose subject is the nature of art.

There are problems either way, and they are deep. Any solution to them must involve the renunciation of some cherished convictions. For the contrast between story and philosophy was also a contrast between time and eternity. Story bound you into the human world of temporal succession and change, whereas philosophy aimed higher, rising above time and story in order to represent genuine knowledge as consisting in the timeless contemplation of the unchangingly and objectively Real. This was a very grandiose idea, and one that religion readily adopted. But from Hegel onwards, as human Reason was increasingly brought down into history and language, knowledge began to be seen less as the timeless contemplation of the unchangingly Real and more as a human life-skill, a practical resource. If we really are animals, then knowledge is for the sake of survival in time. The typical unit of skill-knowledge is not a tenseless concept, but something I shall call an actform, a temporally-extended pattern or form of action. This is just what we were looking for, because it brings knowledge and story very close together. Life is temporal, and stories are also temporally-extended. Story is therefore much more powerfully able to be the actform of life, and to produce life, than is philosophy. If religion is to shape human life, then it has obviously got to take anthropomorphic story-form. So we can rehabilitate myth, as a temporally-extended and life-shaping sort of knowledge. All very well. But as we said, the price is heavy, for this line of thought obviously requires us to abandon the old philosophical and religious dream of absolute, timeless and story-transcending knowledge. That is not easy. It is what has been called the death of God. Are we ready yet for the knowledge, or rather the fiction, that there is no knowledge, and that our religion, and indeed our whole life, is just our fiction?

Maybe we are not yet ready. In recent years there has been a good deal of interest in narrative theology and in a literary approach to the Bible. I am warmly in favour of this develop-ment. But its advocates so far have been distinctly coy about spelling out its full implications. Perhaps this shows prudence on their part. I wish I were prudent too, but I'm not. So here is an account of the world-view we may be led to if our philosophical and religious thinking are to become thoroughly post-metaphysical and literary. I have tried to give the argument a spiralling and narrative shape, so as not to contradict myself too severely.

This is the second of a little group of books that I am calling 'expressionist'. *Creation out of Nothing* appeared in 1990. In this new book I am particularly indebted to Hugh Rayment-Pickard for his criticisms and suggestions.

D.C.

1

WORDS AND TIME

(a) Words out of time

At least since Plato our culture has been deeply influenced by a group of related distinctions which contrast contemplation and action, words and deeds, theory and practice, and pure and applied knowledge. These oppositions seem to imply that the world of knowledge and language may somehow be separated from the world of time and action. Yet this obviously cannot be so, for we live in time, we speak, think and act in time. If knowledge be thought of as a skill or a capacity to get something right, well, the exercise of that skill or capacity takes time. Alternatively, if knowledge be thought of in terms of demonstrably true assertions about what is the case, well, again, sentences take time to utter, as they also take time to hear or peruse. With its subject-verb-object structure, the sentence has already the shape of an action. It may be used to perform an action, or it may evoke, or comment upon or simulate an action. At any rate, a sentence is the intelligible form of an action. It is by being invested with sentences, and guided by sentences, that a bit of physical behaviour becomes a purposeful deed. To act upon a sentence, or even just to understand it, takes time. So the spoken language is completely temporal, the temporally-ordered succession of sounds in a sentence being exactly matched to the succession of motions of the body-forces that run with the sentence, and under its guidance flow out into action.

At least while culture remained oral, based upon the spoken word, this intimate and primal relationship between knowledge, language, action and time could scarcely be lost. Oral culture is transmitted by reciting action-guiding universal narratives –

myths, folk-tales and the like. There is at this stage relatively little speculative or video thought, just because the culture is audio. I dare hazard a guess that the notion of eternity as timelessness is not found either in early childhood or in pre-literate societies. Because writing is visible all-at-once it readily generates metaphors of vision, simultaneity and timelessness, but in an oral culture the myths and other narratives naturally make the gods and spirits speak and act in time exactly as we do. And an oral narrative about a god, when recounted to me, inpinges upon me, stirs my body-forces and affects my feelings exactly as if the god were another human being, just like myself only more so. The gods are archetypal; they set standards for our behaviour. There is no doubt, therefore, that the gods and spirits of oral culture are human and temporal. They live, they act and influence us through language in time. They are as it were big, vivid, fictitious human beings, communal postulates. Admittedly there is not much evidence of them outside language, but the communal postulation of them is nonetheless very powerful. They are potent because their range of symbolic meanings is so wide. They can simultaneously personify cosmic powers, social authority and psychic forces. The narratives about them are known to all, and directly influence our feelings and behaviour so strongly that everything is exactly as if the gods were indeed real superhuman humans. Living in time, living in stories.

In a literate culture, however, an entirely different view of language and time develops. With literacy it becomes possible to write down a sentence and look at it, apparently fixed and simultaneous. A written sentence is no longer tied to a particular moment and circumstances of utterance. It is not merely occasional: it has acquired a certain universality. It stays around, seemingly unchanging, and often surviving the death of its writer. The sentence, which used to be only an occasionally-occurrent temporal form, has now been frozen in writing, spatialized and made general and timeless. Yet it continues, where it is regarded as authoritative, to produce effects in time. Knowledge can now be distinguished from action. It can profess to be concerned with what is timeless and universal, and it can be represented through an all-pervasive metaphoric of vision. So literacy creates a new kind of person, the intellectual, who is in pursuit of a vision of eternal truth and reality.

The visual metaphoric of philosophy includes such terms as theory, vision, speculation, intuition, observation, contemplation, insight, illumination, enlightenment, regard, views, seeing, evidence, manifest and demonstration. I am suggesting that this vocabulary expresses the literate intellectual's confidence in what can be seen laid out before one's eyes, fixed in writing for the scholar to contemplate. In its permanence and universality, the written sign is the forerunner of the platonic Form and the concept.

With writing and philosophy, knowledge therefore becomes tenseless and staticized. The outstanding example of how this happens is Parmenides of Elea (c.510–450 BC), who wrote a long metaphysical poem in hexameters. In the section 'the way of Truth' he deduces the nature of reality by reason alone from the premiss esti, 'it is'. Just by ordering written signs on the page, Parmenides generates a timeless, non-narrative metaphysics of Being. It runs somewhat as follows:

> What is, must be; what is not, cannot be. Most human beings fail sharply to distinguish the two. But we here concern ourselves solely with what is. It is entire, immovable and without end; it is now, all at once, continuous and imperishable. The esti, posited, is always there. There is no void: it fills all things, indivisible and motionless, like a perfect sphere. It is One.[1]

Thus Parmenides worked out, on paper because it *had* to be on paper, the first metaphysics of the Absolute, creating an ideal of knowledge that is anti-narrative, timeless, universal and divorced from action. He has done it just by manipulating the graphic sign esti, and in particular by exploiting the ambiguity between two different uses of esti. For esti can be used existentially to assert that 'It exists' or, differently accented, it may be used just predicatively to say that 'It is something-or-other.' In the arguments there is very frequently a little slip between 'Whatever is, must be something-or-other' and 'What is, must logically be, that is, it must exist necessarily.' Out of that slip, for example in Fr.347,[2] metaphysics grew. Just the way the graphic sign *esti* sat there, unchanging on the page before him, encouraged Parmenides to make the fallacious inference from 'What is, must be determinate' to 'What is, must be absolutely'. The problem lies in the way that the sign itself, just by having been written down, seems to have become objectified, timeless and independent.

Parmenides' fatal presumption, that writing makes a simultaneous and non-narrative vision of truth possible, is illusory. Even written sentences still take time to read. Texts are not really non-temporal, any more than musical scores are. That dubious and too-often-quoted letter in which Mozart supposedly claims to be able to contemplate an entire musical composition simultaneously is nonsensical.[3] In a truly simultaneous vision the order of the notes or movements would have disappeared, which is absurd. A piece of language or a piece of music simply consists in the manner and sequence in which it arouses our body-forces as it moves across the surface of our sensibility. There is no truly non-successive, non-temporal knowledge, or language, or music, or even meaningfulness.

So Parmenides himself must also be telling a sort of story. He creates an impression of having conjured up something absolute and eternal – but he has done so in a *text*, which like every other text is a succession of relativities.

(b) Words in time

'Mortals consider that the gods are born, and that they have clothes and speech and bodies like their own', says Xenophanes of Colophon with some asperity. 'The Ethiopians say their gods are snub-nosed and black, the Thracians that theirs have light blue eyes and red hair.' In such terms the first philosophers ridiculed popular religious belief. It was anthropomorphic and immoral, and the poets were wrong to endorse it. 'Homer and Hesiod have attributed to the gods everything that is a shame and reproach among men, stealing and committing adultery and deceiving each other.'[4]

I am suggesting, however, that in oral, and even in literate, cultures theology cannot help but be narrative. Speech and writing are extended in time. The production of words involves the expenditure of a certain amount of body-force, and hearing or reading them takes time. Words are by cultural training correlated with produced and differentiated bodily feelings. Arranged in a sentence, words are so ordered as to evoke a highly specific and refined play, expression or discharge of feeling. The feeling may run out to form action, or it may be held at the level of simulation. The latter happens in the case of story-telling. So it is that the use of narrative art produces a controlled fantasy or simulation in the hearer, to pleasurable effect.[5]

All this works, however, only because of the huge power of culture to differentiate our feelings, and to establish and maintain an extremely high degree of semantic (which equals emotional) attunement among us. We are superlatively sympathetic creatures, who wish and need intensely to keep in harmony with each other. The resulting intimate socialization of our physiology enables a string of honkings and hootings to generate very much the same simulation in each member of an audience. And in the process of story-telling, as every raconteur knows, the pacing, the order, the rhythm, and the timing of the punch line must all be just right. People are curiously easily emotionally affronted in art and love. When that happens, there is a misfire. One is put off; one goes suddenly cold.

When, however, it all comes right the story mesmerizes the audience, and is in the highest degree entertaining, instructive and edifying. Arousing and discharging feeling, it gives pleasure and heightens vitality. As a narrative simulation, it educates by communicating new actforms to the audience. It produces in the hearer new life-possibilities. A person who has been enthralled by many good stories is equipped with a large stock of actforms to draw upon as she subsequently tries to make narrative sense of her own life. That is why we tell children stories. That is why 'the mind' is *made* of stories. That is why in every situation in life we must draw upon our stock of actforms in order to find a way of making an intelligible story out of what is going on around us, and what we ourselves are going to do about it. Finally, the great stories are edifying in the sense of community-building. If there is a body of communal stories that we all know, then we can together draw upon them to construct a meaningful public life in which we all participate and sympathize.

All this suggests a perfectly straightforward sense in which 'all is fiction', and in which there are and have to be national and religious myths about heroic deeds and gods. But the stories won't work unless the gods and heroes are fully as human as we are ourselves. The stories about the gods have to engage our human feelings in human temporal sequences, and they must supply us with humanly-usable actforms. Gods and heroes are and must be archetypal humans, performing archetypal deeds and drawing us into their life.

It is all highly temporal, and I have also been hinting that time in language is physiological. We are not just talking about heartbeats, paces and circadian rhythms. Nor are we just talking about the rhythms of activity and rest, hunger and satisfaction, wakefulness and sleep. More than that, we are talking about sex; about the various delicate and interesting considerations of order, rhythm, pace, timing and the general orchestration of events towards a climax. I'm saying that all the rules about effective timing are just the same in the two cases – as seducers know. Storytelling is a kind of seduction.

So the gods of Greece and India do indeed behave just like human beings, 'stealing and committing adultery' as Xenophanes sniffily says. Quite so. A sentence is a sequence oriented towards a target. It gathers a force and directs it towards a specific object.[6] In even and well-paced prose, the blow falls rhythmically in sentence after sentence, building up the pressure. Furthermore, the subject-verb-object structure, in which the verb may be active or passive, clearly indicates the sexual metaphor that language cannot help but be. Sentences generate, reflect, guide and finish processes, events and actions. They thereby shape reality, and indeed in many languages the word used for sentence is used also to mean legal or moral pronouncement or decision, commandment, and what I am calling actform. In a double sense, words *order*: they both arrange and ordain.

The philosophers rebelled against the old oral narrative culture. By giving precedence to the contemplation of truth fixed in writing, they turned the old temporal order into a simultaneous spatial one. Practice was replaced by theory, and actforms by timeless concepts. Stories about the gods were replaced by speculation about the nature of things. The old narrative-emotional engagement with the living of life was set aside in favour of a new ascetical ideal of disinterested and visionary knowledge, absolute knowledge, oddly disjoined from the imagination, the emotions and action. Fittingly, almost all the great philosophers from Plato to Kant were unmarried. Their ideal of knowledge had become celibate. It was also very staticized, oriented towards an unchanging realm of self-identical concepts or essences. Thinkers in the platonic tradition have always found it oddly difficult to get their vocabulary to describe the way things and ideas change through time.

Ironically, platonism also ran into paradoxes on its chosen home ground. Philosophy seemed to pretend to be able to transcend the world of language, time and narrative. Yet the philosophers themselves composed sentences; how else could they communicate to us their dream of timeless and sentence-transcending rational intuition? Thus their message was contradicted by the medium, namely language, in which they had to express it. The only way to hide the contradiction was to make the medium transparent to the point of invisibility, so that nobody would notice it. It was therefore claimed that philosophy doesn't use rhetoric but only pure argument, and that it does not fiction or entertain, but puts everything in the very plainest and clearest prose. Philosophy assures us that it never ever cheats: its language is so clear, non-rhetorical and non-narrative that we can take it on trust and disregard it. Every philosopher said by implication: 'I'm not telling tales. Trust me. My language is invisible. Look straight through it, please.' But the philosophers did tell stories, even if only stories about how we their readers could come to share their point of view. And not only is argument itself a form of rhetoric, but also close examination reveals that the great philosophical texts are fictioned and fabricated just as craftily as any other works of art.

It is evident now – isn't it? – that the philosophical tradition is a line of texts, a literary tradition, and that all those dreams of 'transcending' language and time and metaphor are just metaphors that can't help but remain within language and time. 'Eternal' is a trisyllable that takes time to produce, and 'Absolute' just a part of the system of relativities that is language. Obvious, surely. Yet if so, if philosophy was nothing but a literary genre, a fiction, then what had been the point of it?

It was all for the sake of making enlightened and critical thinking possible. The asceticism, the attempt to become completely disengaged, the distinction between appearance and Reality, the pretension to linguistic transparency and the claim that one could rise to view things as a whole from the standpoint of eternity – all this was part of an apparatus for self-schooling that did on the whole a good job, in its day. But now philosophy, including religious and ethical thinking, needs to return into language and time. Its home, where it really belongs.

(c) Words and deeds

Language is most at home and runs along most smoothly when it is interwoven with human action. It may be producing and regulating the action, it may be following and describing it, or it may just be telling a story; but however thay may be, language does action better than it does anything else. Consider for example the way a sports reporter, less than a second behind the events, produces a quickfire running commentary on a football game. He accomplishes this feat with such fluency that it is as though the action were coming at him already formed into sentence-shapes, and turning it into words were almost an automatic process. And that is in fact our doctrine, for I am saying that the commentator actually sees a proper name verbing the adjectival ball to another proper name. Language shapes the way the players frame their play and the way the commentator sees what's happening. We see the world in terms of syntax and the parts of speech. It's a language-shaped world, and that is why we can turn it into words so readily.

There is a further indication of the languagey character of

what is going on at the football game. It is a rule-governed, highly symbolic activity like a conversation or a debating contest. The players pass the ball to each other as on other occasions we pass the metaphorical ball in one of our language-games, and they try to deny the other side possession much as we may try to exclude somebody from a conversation. The ball is what in the case of conversation may be called the initiative or the point. Interposing to take possession is much the same in conversation as in football. You just barge in, right? So metaphors from conversation infiltrate sport – 'He's got no answer to that,' we may say when somebody's beaten. Metaphors from sport similarly infiltrate conversation: 'The ball is in your court.'

Now perform some sequence of physical actions yourself, giving a full running commentary on what you are doing as you do it. The commentary has a clarifying and enhancing effect, like the black outline used by a number of Post-Impressionist painters. Telling yourself what you are doing as you do it helps you directly to apprehend the action-forming power of language. It literally *describes* the world by drawing black outlines around things and events, and thereby produces action as publicly-intelligible conduct. Language gives form to what is happening.

Some years ago the organizers of sporting events began to notice that many people in the crowd liked to listen on their portable radios to a simultaneous commentary upon an event at which they were present. The commentary still helps, even if you are there. Accordingly the organizers nowadays often arrange for a continuous running commentary to be broadcast by loudspeaker to the crowd at a big meeting. What is happening in such a case? Certainly the commentary explains what's going on and names the competitors, but there is more to it than that. Through its power over our emotions language makes us participants in what it describes. We identify with one competitor or another, and this very strong self-identification with the competitor that takes us right out of ourselves is what the spectators have paid for. It is what they call having a good time.

Evidently we have a very intense desire to identify emotionally with a team or competitor, so that their struggle, their victory or defeat is ours. A philosophical tradition that for millennia praised reason and self-mastery still inclines us to despise ourselves for this passionate desire to get away from our selves and identify with others. We call it weakness or escapism, a failure of self-possession and self-control. Yet I am suggesting that human life cannot work unless we are all of us somewhat vicarious and multi-personal. We all live out a variety of stories through a variety of *personae* real and fictitious, with our stories often interwoven and overlapping. I am not a single self; I am a tangle of tales. I am many selves, and not all of them are my own.

Returning to the sporting commentary, let us now remove the events, and keep only the soundtrack. The capacity of the words to stir our feelings remains unaffected. The words alone are sufficient. Indeed, I maintain that a particular use of a word just is the activation of a feeling, a meaning being nothing but a feeling culturally-scaled and linked by association with other feelings. After all, a phonic signifier, a heard word, is nothing but a noise. So there is nothing for the meaning of a word to be, except its material effect upon our physiology. The impinging sound provokes a feeling-response and various learned associations. That's all there is; but it is enough. The heard commentary affects me just as if I were at the match. I start to get emotionally involved, which means that I lock on to the individual or the team that I support.

The same happens in straight fiction. We never read a novel or see a film without identifying ourselves with a leading character, often, but by no means always, a person of the same sex as oneself. Evidently there is a sense in which we are all actors: we love to play at being other, imaginary people.

Now what is the point of these simulations and fictions that bulk so large in our lives? They are not just idle dreams or rehearsals for action. They are rather more than a way of exploring possible alternative selves. It seems that to produce a life, I need not just a well-stocked mind and not just a large repertoire of actforms, but also a well-peopled mind. I need a very big stock of characters, roles, costumes, emblematic and allegorical figures, the bigger the better, and I will use this stock not only in constructing my own behaviour but also in building my theories about what other people are getting up to. In a way that philosophy has on the whole too much neglected, I have to be multi-personal because my consciousness has to be as it were spread over a large number of other people besides myself. I can't shape my life among them unless I have a pretty good idea of how they tick, and I also need a good range of possible selves for myself to be in response to the tricks they get up to. I cannot write my life simply in straight expository prose; I have to rough out the production script for a whole drama, in which my own voice is just one amongst a number of others. We all need to have in us something of the imaginative powers not only of the actor but also of the novelist or dramatist. We have got to be able to imagine an entire social world and the way it moves, its 'theatrics', before we can set about constructing our own lives within it.

The first philosopher to say that consciousness has evolved not just to enable us to understand ourselves, but rather in order to enable us to get inside other people and imagine what they may be like and how we may expect them to behave, was Nietzsche. However, Nietzsche also saw that since signs are general, the notions about character-types that we must use cannot help but be stereotypes. Brutally, he says that consciousness must unavoidably be something 'shallow, thin, relatively stupid, general, sign, herd signal'.[7] Think of the conventional character-types to be found in a Rossini opera, a Chaplin comedy or a Grimm Brothers fairy tale. Herd stereotypes, every one of them. Equally banal are the animal emblems, the lists of virtues and vices, and the saints and sinners of much popular moralizing.

Thus far Nietzsche's clearly right. Consciousness is indeed a disaster insofar as it leads people to posit and live by cliché-characters. We do indeed tend to make clichés of ourselves and of other people. You and I know very well that we have ourselves dropped into the most ludicrous cliché-behaviour when we have been in the grip of strong emotions such as offended pride, sexual love or jealousy. We have found ourselves behaving with truly operatic absurdity. But the novelist's art and the use of the imagination in the moral life ought constantly to be working against the tyranny of stereotypes. Art is always a little irregular. It must be so, to avoid the numbness and boredom created by unthinking repetition and set patterns. Art cannot be just predictable. Furthermore, some non-naturalistic narratives such as fairy tales, myths and religious stories are so highly symbolic that they resist any crude or mechanical acting-out. Their influence upon us is more pervasive and subtle.

All this sheds light upon an interesting paradox. Religion, after telling us a story, says: 'Go and do thou likewise.' Its teachings are to be acted upon, turned into conduct. And in particular there is a very long tradition, going back to St Paul's letters and to the gospels, of urging believers to imitate Christ. Yet only with qualifications. Crudely 'literal' imitation of Christ was not approved of. You were not to court martyrdom quite so openly as he had seemingly done, and there has never been a report of anyone actually going to the area of Galilee south-west of the Lake, and there taking up the life of an itinerant preacher.

What would be wrong with an attempt exactly to copy Jesus' life? St Paul's answer seems to be that the religious actform or story pattern that you live by should shape your life only at the most general level. You should come down from Heaven, you should take up your cross, you should be poor and so on – but only metaphorically.[8] Slavish copying is simply not conduct. There would be something absurd and even irreligious about trying to live exactly like Jesus. Even when it was at its most authoritarian, our religious tradition was aware that its various narratives and rules cannot wholly relieve us of the responsibility for writing the story of our own lives. The life of Christ may show me how to live, but it cannot simply be adopted as my own life. That is not its function. And in any case the fluid, multi-faceted character of religious myths and stories ensures that they influence different people in different ways.

(d) The point of stories

We know little or nothing either about the mental life of the people who first composed and heard folktales and myths, or about the settings in which such traditional stories were originally told. They have reached us simply as texts and are almost free-floating. Yet they are important cultural products which presumably have a meaning. It is not surprising therefore that some critics have thought it best to treat them formalistically, as crypts. The text of the story is reduced to a kind of static algebra, a diagram to be analysed and decoded. Vladimir Propp[9] and Claude Lévi-Strauss[10] are the two best-known writers of this type. Their procedure inevitably finds in the story a rather abstract and general cultural message.

It seems to me that this approach leaves too much out. It omits the temporally-extended dynamic movement of stories, and the correlation they maintain between the flowing movement of the feelings that they prompt and the goings-on in the external world that they describe.

For example, many or most stories have always included such plot-themes as the following:

pilgrimage → goal
desire → satisfaction
struggle → victory, success
opposition → mediation
conflict → resolution
bound → free
lost → found
problem → solution,
  etc.

We may call these simple and universal narrative patterns *mythemes*, a term introduced by Lévi-Strauss. A story may elaborate just one of them or incorporate a whole series of them. And notice that each mytheme has a psychological inside to it, and a behavioural outside. Subjectively, the narrative evokes feelings of desire seeking satisfaction, fears seeking abatement, tension seeking relief. The emotional music that the narrative generates in the hearer is very like that which is aroused by the Romantic symphony. But at the same time the narrative also conjures up a movement of events in the outside world through which our feelings can be relieved, gratified or purged.

In the telling, the story is an unfolding syntagmatic chain of signs. The storyteller recites it, and the leading edge of the narrative moves along like the slider of a zip fastener, continuously interlocking a movement of aroused feelings in the hearer and a movement of referred-to events in the world. So the story in the telling opens up and explores possible forms of life, by suggesting how mythemes synchronize our own psychology with objective reality. Here, it says, are ways in which feeling and living can flow together. *Contra* Freud, every story suggests that there does not have to be a head-on permanent collision between the pleasure-principle and the reality-principle. Our feelings can make, or find, the world they want.

The child demands to know, 'Is the story going to be about me?' – and of course it is. Stories teach life. They show us to be metaphorical animals whose medium is the sign. The movement of signs continuously produces both the inner world and the outer, and keeps them in concert.

Narratives don't just provide forms[11] for my action; being multi-charactered, they also teach interaction. They advise and warn us as to how other people may be expected to behave towards us, and they teach interactive social skills. Children's stories concentrate especially on preparing children to cope with the cruelty and the incomprehensibly malignant power-games of adults. Riddle and Trickster stories teach repartee, the importance of low cunning and the skills of survival. And so on.

The intense pleasure stories give us is the pleasure of metaphor and metonymy. By prompting us to compare and contrast the like and the unlike, the similar and the dissimilar, and by teaching us to look out for and take pleasure in analogies and correspondences within the field of experience, metaphor makes us intelligent. That much is obvious. Our heavily spatialized intellectual heritage makes it rather less easy to recognize something else equally important, namely the fact that metonymy (the pursuit of meaning down a chain of signifiers) makes it possible for us to live and act. For metonymy, moving from word to word and building up meaning, makes possible the recognition of a temporally-unfolding intelligible order of things, something philosophy always had difficulty in recognizing.

The first thing metonymy helps make possible is just syntax itself: the recognition of the way each and every one of the words in a well-crafted sentence, occurring in just that order, fits so beautifully together to create the unified force of the fully-accumulated sentence. Syntax then opens up the equally-beautiful and amazing way in which a series of human actions, performed in just the right order, may fit together to accomplish a single purpose. And the third thing metonymy makes possible is a good story, *which unifies the first two*, and proves that the coherence and intelligibility of our life is nothing other than the coherence and intelligibility of our language. The movement from word to word gathers the force of meaning that makes intelligible expression possible.

Thus a good religious story may persuade me that it is possible for me so to live that I can make my life make sense. And religion itself is the attempt so to live as to make life make sense, whatever happens. It says: 'In spite of everything, we can make a meaningful life out of the struggle against meaningless-ness.' And that's the only answer there will ever be to the so-called 'problem of evil'. Religious rituals and stories help us so to live that we find psychic fulfilment in creative and expressive action. That *is* the conquest of evil and despair.

The pleasure of stories, then, is the pleasure of the metaphors that make us intelligent and the metonymies that enable us to live meaningful lives in time. Often the two principles work together. In children's fairy stories ogres and wicked step-mothers take the place of fathers and nothers. We recognize in such a case that the substitution of one word for another veils things, and so makes it possible to handle various painful, difficult or forbidden topics. The initial metonymic substitution – for example, of witch for mother – opens the flow of narrative. From now on the syntax of the sentence and the orderly unfolding of a familiar story guides and controls feelings that might otherwise become too strong to be bearable. And, rather contrary to what Freud may have led us to expect, the young child takes additional pleasure in being ironically aware of the joke. That is, the child recognizes that fearsome objects such as parents are concealed behind witches and giants, and that fearsome emotions are released in a managed way by the unfolding of the story. When, for example, we read Goldilocks and the Three Bears[12] to a small child, we use a deep voice for the big bear, a medium voice for the middle bear and a squeaky voice for the little bear. This makes it easy for the child to see that the story is about a small child's efforts to find its own proper place in the hierarchy of the family, and about the same child's frequent experience of being told off for trespassing upon somebody else's territory. The child to whom we tell the story gets the joke, and enjoys the quasi-sexual pleasure of uncovering a secret combined with the conspiratorial pleasure of sharing it, unspoken, with the storyteller.

But the greatest delight of story is yet to come. Art creates life. That is, the movement of the signs in the story stirs our feelings, seduces us, brings us to life, makes and orders a world for us. In *Life Lines* (1986) I still followed Schopenhauer and Freud in supposing that Nature precedes Culture. First there is the upwelling natural force of the Will (or Libido, or feeling or 'the productive life-energy') and secondly there are the culturally-provided channels through which it can express itself. Telling a story, then, is like opening a safety-valve or turning on a tap. The life-energy seeks discharge; it needs symbols to help it flow out into representation or expression. In *The Long-Legged Fly* (1988) I modified that account, trying instead to keep desire and the sign exactly in step. Neither was to be given precedence. Culture and Nature were the upper and lower faces of a ripple running over a single depthless surface.

Now – being older, perhaps – I am at last really ready to admit that language comes first, and story comes first. By awakening our senses and the movement of our feelings, art produces life. The Sleeping Beauty is a story about stories. Story's kiss wakes us up, produces desire, produces reality.

(e) Story and the production of desire

A very long tradition inclines us to believe in something called Nature. We think there is a natural order of things out there, determinate, independent of and prior to Culture. Nature is seen as fully in place and functioning more or less autonomously *before* Culture comes along and builds upon it.

A view of this type sees culture as artificial, secondary and inessential. It is related to nature pretty much as clothing is to the body. Fine clothing may adorn and enhance the body, it may be very comfortable; but after all, the body is a complete functioning system without it. We tend to associate nakedness with truth, and clothing with deception. So Nature is truth.

If nature can thus exist prior to culture, we may suppose there could be such a being as a 'natural man'. This being might be seen as a bundle of biological needs and drives which keep building up and seeking expression or gratification. Just by trial and error, he might discover the behaviour-patterns that enable him to meet his needs and to remain in balance. A successful discharge of accumulated tension might open a neural pathway in his brain, so that he could learn by practice. He might also be able to respond promptly and appropriately, either by reflex action or by learned behaviours, to a wide range of sensory stimuli.

Such a being would be a living, functioning human animal. He would require very little, if anything, in the way of either culture or consciousness. And something very like him has been imagined both by Thomas Hobbes, and by the Freud of the outline *Project for a Scientific Psychology* (1895).

Various striking assumptions are being made by models of this type. The psychology is dynamic: we are regarded as active beings powered by strong, continuously up-welling drives. These drives are numerous and very specific. We have to find and learn the precise outlets, symbols or behaviour-patterns through which alone they can find satisfaction. If for whatever reason they are denied their natural expression they will find substitute hallucinatory fulfilment, for example in dreams.

What is wrong with these assumptions can be stated very briefly. Nobody has ever located and measured the instinctual drives in the brain, or found where their energy is stored up. They have nowhere been definitively listed and distinguished from each other, because they cannot be. Human tastes and preferences in matters of food and drink, sex, phobias and so forth are so very highly specific, so plastic, so easily displaced and so obviously relative to what culture currently provides, that they cannot plausibly be separated from culture and put in a different box marked 'Nature'. In fact our emotions, like our gender-roles, are complex cultural formations and have histories. For example, we have a large number of highly conventionalized cinematic genres such as the thriller, the horror film, the comedy thriller, the crime caper, the chase thriller and the detective film. These genres all have histories, including prehistories in literature. They are correlated with highly specific emotions. People go to a thriller to be thrilled in a very distinctive way. From the way a Hitchcock film works it is evident that the thriller does not merely release a pre-existent pent-up natural emotion, but is so constructed as to produce and to play upon a culturally-formed emotion. And in fact from Freud's own text, and especially in his ideas about dreams and jokes, it is evident that for him our unconscious emotional life is *not* purely biological, but is transacted in our native language and in cultural symbols. So the unconscious is cultural and not natural. Otherwise put, culture or socialization goes all the way down. A purely natural level of human psychic life is never reached, just as nobody has ever produced 'the natural man'.

Works of art, then, do not function merely to supply outlets for inbuilt and already-determinate natural feelings. Their job is rather to *produce* our feelings, differentiate them and attach symbolic values to them. As Wagner noted in his programmatic writings about music-drama, such artforms seem to achieve their greatest expressive emotional power when they are multi-media. Opera and cinema mix visual narrative with dramatic text and musical accompaniment or setting. *Tristan and Isolde* shows what emotional intensity opera can achieve, while an accomplished chase thriller is the most exquisitely cinematic sort of cinema.

So we are queuing outside the cinema, not in order to be purged, but to be turned on. We do not say to ourselves: 'I feel a certain specific desire at such-and-such a strength, so I must seek out just the right genre of entertainment to relieve that desire.' Rather, we hope to be excited, turned on, aroused, entertained and taken out of ourselves. Art exists to be a stimulant, an aphrodisiac rather than merely a form of relief massage. Art's job is to create life. It proffers symbolic forms which seduce our feelings, drawing them out into expression. A feeling that has been pulled out into a form thereafter remains associated with that form. Thus art shapes our emotional life.

We desire to desire; but far from being insatiably randy animals, we need to be coaxed into desire. Very often we are sluggish and difficult. Tricks and techniques are needed in order to get us going: a touch of spice or incongruity like a beauty spot, a touch of alienation or distancing, as when a man spies on his own wife, or a touch of symbolic concealment which like a figleaf or a fan draws attention by hiding. Of all such artistic devices story is one of the most powerful. The technical craft of the story teller, like that of the film editor and the seducer, is the craft of building up, sustaining and pacing an emotional development.

(f) Story and the production of reality

Like a melody, like a film sequence, and like indeed just the sound of a voice, a story may arouse our feelings and play a kind of sustained tune upon them. Story helps to produce and to differentiate subjectivity, which is why in our modern culture it still remains so very important. That is relatively easy to understand; but it is much harder to get clear about just how a story produces an objective world, whether real or imaginary.

Here is a superficial, but at least clear, line of thought which gives us an entry to the problem.

In March 1990, a few months ago at the time of writing, there was a major political demonstration in London. Even before it took place many people were already beginning to prepare their stories about what was going to happen, and what its political significance would be. In the event it was a distinctly lively day, with a good deal of fighting, many injuries, much damage and over five hundred arrests. Even while the event was taking place rival stories about it were pouring out from the police, the organizers, the politicians, the news media and various young people in the crowd. Next day the event had become a great tangle of competing stories, jostling fiercely against each other. As I write the arguments are still going on, because there are so many conflicting interests involved. The police do not want the events to be officially declared a riot, or they may face claims from the owners of damaged property, and the competence of their commanders on the day may come under public scrutiny. The politicians are still trying to blame each other, for the events were filmed live and flashed around the world, doing the present Government's overseas reputation no good at all. Young people charged by the police are still telling their stories in magistrates' courts.

In a case like this we become aware of the way what people call history evolves over the weeks and the years as the provisional outcome of a contest of stories.[13] Sometimes a public enquiry or Royal Commission is used by way of trying to establish a predominant story of what happened, but an event such as a political demonstration is far too complex and controversial for there to be such a thing as the Truth about it. A fresh enquiry by a journalist or historian may at any time upset the received account. And so it is with every facet of modern life. Reality is a battlefield, an endless struggle between many rival stories about what's going on. Truth is the state of the argument, truth is the story on top at present, truth is a precarious and always shifting consensus. At *best*.

Now we begin to see the point of stories. Stories show us that we have the task of constructing our own lives as narratives, and they start to teach us how we can do it. But stories also show us that we live in a multipersonal world with many different angles and interests. We have to carve out our own life-stories in alliance or in competition with other people who are trying to do the same. Truth is struggle, truth is plural, truth's a survival skill – so stories tell us by their very form. 'The novel,' declares Salman Rushdie in one of his apologies for it, 'has always been *about* the way in which different languages, values and narratives quarrel, and about the shifting relations between them, which are relations of power. The novel does not seek to establish a privileged language, but it insists upon the freedom to portray and analyse the struggle between the different contestants for such privileges.'[14]

So the reality that stories produce is an arena over which different stories struggle for supremacy, a space in which different people are attempting in their various ways to make their own lives make sense. In the process they understand and misunderstand each other, co-operate and compete, join hands and part company, find happiness or disaster. To learn about all this is to learn a practical wisdom of life – and that is what stories teach.

So far, so good. Fairy tale, drama and fiction exist to teach us that getting along with other people is about nine-tenths of the problem of life. Until we have got at least some competence in that area, we can do nothing at all. In retrospect it is odd that the great theories of knowledge, especially those produced between Descartes and Kant, should have paid so little attention to other people. How do we come to recognize that they are there at all, and how can we construct decent working hypotheses about how the world appears to them, and what they are trying to do?

Philosophy's historic blindness in this area was inbuilt. Ever since Plato it had privileged unity, the unity and self-sufficiency of the self and the ideal unity of a fully-systematized body of knowledge. From the first, therefore, it tended to represent knowledge as a solitary achievement. Then at the Renaissance the viewpoint for philosophy became, more than ever before, that of the solitary human subject. Like a Florentine painter looking over a point and through a strung-frame grid, Descartes set out to take a deliberately one-eyed and solipsistic view of the world. By contrast, the fiction writer since very early times has been acutely aware of the many different and partial angles from which life's action can be viewed. The narrator's eye that views the action may view it as past or as present, may view it from an omniscient or from a finite standpoint, and may be the eye of any one of the characters or none of them. But this means that the dramatist and fiction-writer, for the sake of the craft, is and has to be somewhat plural as a person – and, what's more, holds that it is a good thing to be plural. You need to be plural because reality is multiple and because you need to be able to get inside other people's skins.

Thus, just as a matter of literary genre, philosophy until perhaps Kierkegaard was always one-eyed, whereas story-telling is in principle multi-perspectival.

Now we may be ready to dig a spit deeper. A story is only a linear chain of signs, very like a piece of music in the way it produces a linear series of firings in my nervous system, or a linear series of ripples spreading over the surface of my sensibility. How do we get from story as a linear chain of feeling-events to story as simulation of a very complex inter-personal world? Just whistle to yourself in a tuneless, jerky sort of a way for a minute. Now ask yourself, how does stuff like *that* become a multi-perspectival world?

The answer is given by grammar and syntax. They alone prescribe how we must construct our world. The major constituents and relations to be found in the world are given by the parts of speech, the declensions of nouns and the conjugations of verbs. Skill in using the indexical pronouns I, me, you and so forth correctly, and in grasping the way in which their reference moves around according to who is using them, supplies the idea of a multipersonal world with many shifting angles. The active and passive voices of verbs give us the idea of a world in which we both act and get acted upon. As soon as I start to learn language I am made to learn the difference between sentences that I have myself initiated, and sentences initiated from outside myself. As soon as I have even the most modest degree of skill with language, I am already within the world of stories, the human world.

(g) Good and bad stories

Since the rise of Western philosophy, narrative, change and the passage of time have always been regarded as bad for truth. Truth that has become fully temporalized has been considered liable to erosion and leakage. It seeps away. So strongly was this felt that the traditional formal logic of propositions remained present-tense-only until modern times. The assumption was that truth and certainty could only be held firm if propositions and the logical relationships between them were kept suspended in a timeless present. As soon as change came in, certainty flew out of the window.

When people think this way, how can there be truth in stories? The standard answer went like this: the temporal successiveness of the story, in the reading or the telling of it, admittedly cannot be the vehicle of truth. But the story completed, like a finished painting, may be able to function as an allegory of timeless truth. The finished story as an icon, set-piece or tableau is not quite itself the truth, but it can serve as a symbol of the truth. And if the truth signified is thus something quite distinct from the sign that signifies it, then the sign as such is only instrumental. It is not itself the holy thing. So you may have a good deal of freedom to retell the story or to embroider it, if thereby you can better bring out the unchanging, non-narrative truth that the story is trying to point to. In the older pre-Enlightenment culture artists and preachers usually saw themselves not as pure innovators, but as craftsmen reworking traditional stories and themes. Yet they had a good deal of freedom to reinterpret, because the Real Truth signified, the truth you dared not touch, was not located within the movement of the mere signs. It was outside the text, and the text only bore witness to it.

When however, as has happened with us, truth fully returns into time, narrative and the movement of language, the interpreter's task begins to look very different. Truth is no longer something self-identical, unchanging and subsisting outside the text, but — as we can all feel in great writing like Joyce's — is inherent in the very motion of the signs that compose the text. Truth is no longer something out there; it is a way of words. The preacher, interpreter or artist is now making truth in the telling of the tale. Truth is no longer held firm and self-identical in eternity; instead, it lives and grows and changes in time.[15] The interpreter's job becomes one of creating new truth, by letting the old signs move around and drop into new and fertile relationships. The interpreter is no longer just a servant of the Truth, but has become someone whose job is the endless production of truth. Truth is like music and love; it has to flow continually. Out of us, like living water.

In consequence of all this, we replace the old notion of an immutable Truth out there with a new notion of truth as something more like a quality of flowing life-in-time which is immanent in certain movements of signs or narratives. Good stories produce it in us, enriching us. And the question of the criteria for discriminating between good stories and bad ones now takes a new form, and becomes very important.

The best guide we have in this area is the metaphors in ordinary language. They suggest that when we get into a rut or drop into a fixed routine, we begin to die. Our appetite for life or libido needs to be sustained by continual – even if usually only minor and gradual – change and difference. We simply must have that little bit of innovation, incongruity, blemish or surprise to turn us on. This is as true of work and religion as it is of sex. Thus the job of any cultural worker, whether artist, preacher or entertainer, is always to find a new metaphor, to turn things around, and to cause people's eyes to widen.

We are not talking about mere sensationalism, but about the extent to which in any cultural tradition change is the condition of life (a familiar principle, by the way, in physiology). As an example, consider the celebrated first performance of Igor Stravinsky's 'The Rite of Spring' in 1913. The audience felt insulted. Stravinsky, for his part, would make no concessions. Consciously iconoclastic, he liked to say that he was trying to expel from music just about everything that Romanticism had prized in it. In retrospect the original audience reaction seems absurd; but then, Stravinsky's own claims seem overstated too. He has himself now become part of the canon, and his music seems to us easy, rhythmic, tuneful and joyous. How are we to characterize both the shock his early works originally caused, and their subsequent normalization? I reply that Stravinsky was extending the limits of what people's sensibility was then prepared to accept as being rhythmic, or melodious. No doubt his first audiences found his work painful and difficult to listen to. But we have learnt to accept it. By pushing back the limits Stravinsky enhanced our ability to make or to recognize patterns of meaningfulness within experience. Musical patterns are cognitive; they are emotion-forms, and so incipiently thought-forms and act-forms. By increasing the range of musical patterns we can accept and put to use, Stravinsky enhances life and strengthens the culture.

When genre fiction, poetry and music become too smooth, regular and predictable we are sickened. We do not want the melody to flow too sweetly, the happy ending to be seen coming, or the beat to become too even. Art must intrude upon us and induce us to accept a certain amount of irregularity, jaggedness and syncopation. If it succeeds in this, the feeling of enhanced life is that much the greater. The metrical and rhythmic irregularities in Shakespeare's verse are not faults that the ear tolerates, but artistic necessities. Mere regularity is not art.

Genre fiction cannot be great art because it is too predictable and too much committed to its own conventions. It is written to a formula, a market. When we buy it, there is an implicit understanding that we are not going to have our expectations confounded. We'll get the conclusion we want. Genre fiction has promised to be easy, whereas art is always a little difficult, a little transgressive. It does not conform to our expectations, but challenges our very notion of form, and thereby enhances life.

On the older platonic account, forms are unchanging intelligible essences. On the account I am proposing they are story-like. They are temporally-extended patterns or sequences; they are cultural structures, produced and taught to us especially by art and religion, and they equip us to overcome chaos, order experience and shape our lives.[16] Indeed they may be said actually to produce life. And they need continually to be reinvented and renewed. The admirable British use of 'the other' to mean 'sex' is a reminder that we always need a little bit of novelty or difference to pique us, and turn us on. All products, routines and performances need now and again a little spice of otherness to refresh them, or they go stale. As for truth, the truth that rings true and is true to life, narrative truth, truth in time – we see it as a sort of life-enhancing zest or sparkiness in the way signs move. Art-truth, therefore.

(h) Stories and the production of time

What makes a particular series of notes into a melody – or at least a musical passage? What makes a particular series of dance movements into an intelligible piece of mimed narrative? What makes a row of three or four drawn cartoon frames into a readable strip? What makes a chain of sentences, introducing perhaps several different characters, into an episode in a story? And what makes a particular series of shots in film, duly cut and joined up, into an effective sequence?

In these cases our linguistic idioms give us a first clue. A sequence needs to be *effective*, it must *work*, it must *get somewhere*, it must *produce* a certain dramatic effect, and there must be some sort of narrative *build-up*. Evidently the components of the sequence must be so ordered that they progressively accumulate a certain force of meaning or emotional tension that contributes to moving the whole narrative along. This progressive accumulation gives the direction of time's arrow, for in a sequence there is not just succession but also progression. The sequence runs in one direction only. Thus the question: 'What is a sequence?' is in effect the question: 'What is a story?' asked from the point of view of time. We are asking what makes a row of sayings, steps, sounds or pictures hang together in a form which we recognize as narrative time, the time of our human life.

Two paradoxes stick out at once. The first is the danger of circular definition. Asking ourselves what makes this row of items hang together as a narrative, we think for a moment about how the detective in a classical detective story weaves together a lot of disparate scraps into a narrative hypothesis about how the original crime could have been committed. So here the scraps hang together insofar as the detective is able to weave them into a plausible story. But if we apply this example to our present question, we will merely produce a circular definition. We will be saying that the reason why the elements in a narrative sequence hang together in an intelligible, one-directional temporal order is that we can make a story out of them. Which is in effect to define story in terms of itself. That's no use. We already *know* that we have a sequence, a meaningful bit of narrative. The question is, what makes it all hang together, and how does it manage to produce our human sort of linear, accumulating, 'historical' time?

The question is not easy, because of the second paradox I have to point out. It is that modern art has been a continual self-overcoming. That is, it works away restlessly at stretching or subverting whatever happens to be the current definition of itself. It actively resists being pinned down. Thus it is well known that directors of thrillers, when editing film sequences, must use imagery and pacing with mathematical precision in order to create a slow-burning build-up of tension. This may lead us to think that a theory of what a film sequence is and how it works must be possible. The director of genre cinema is after all using carefully-calculated techniques to produce something like a conditioned reflex response from the audience. Surely these techniques can be rationalized? But no, it seems that they cannot. The history of the cinema shows continual development of narrative and editing techniques. In the work of some current directors such as Martin Scorsese we see the editors trying to get away with ever-more-outrageously-wide jump-cuts, as if they are deliberately setting out to pique and to challenge the audience, or saying that the rules are only there to be broken. You cannot hope to set limits in advance to what film editors may be able to get away with, for as soon as you specify the limits it will immediately become necessary to try to find a way round them. But if you cannot in the traditional philosophical manner fix limits to the range of possible answers to the question of what is a sequence, then the corollary is that you'll never succeed in specifying what the essential characteristics of any sequence have to be.

To give a second example, much more briefly: many operatic arias, and indeed much Romantic music, build up emotion to a sexual climax in the manner of Isolde's *Liebestod*. Again, we may think we have here the starting-point for an agreeably clear and straightforward Freudian theory of how sequences work. They are grounded in human physiology. The *Liebestod* is a chain of expressive signs that give Isolde and her audience succession, steady rhythm, and a linear progressive build-up to a climactic discharge of emotion. Around this classic example we can then elaborate a theory of the dynamics of narrative, of time and of desire. Unfortunately, however, much of twentieth-century music has quite deliberately distanced itself from any such theory of what music is and how it works. A theory of sequence based on Wagner or Verdi will not help us to understand Harrison Birtwhistle, or even Peter Maxwell Davies.

Our two paradoxes are, then, first that it is only too easy to find oneself giving a circular answer to the question of what makes a sequence a sequence; and secondly that art in any case seems continually to subvert any over-easy definition of itself.

So I admit that, especially in avant-garde work, there are sure to be exceptions even to the very general account I am going to give. Nevertheless, I propose the thesis that (almost) every sequence is found to fulfil three conditions, and by fulfilling them creates time. The conditions are (*i*) that in any sequence there will be a play of continuity and discontinuity; (*ii*) that sequences work in one direction only, thus creating Time's arrow; and (*iii*) that in sequences there is always some way in which Time is made 'visible', either by varying the pace of the work, or by contrasting the work's own internal time-scale with the audience's time, or in some other way. Thus sequences produce temporal succession, Time's arrow, and the strange elasticity and relativity of human time that makes it possible for us to *think* time and so to have ideas about the past and the future.

All this must be spelled out in a little more detail.

(*i*) First, then, a sequence requires both continuity and difference. Without continuity there is no connectedness, and therefore no sequence and no story. But without some elements of discontinuity there is no progression, and therefore no sequence and no story. Each newly-arriving unit in a sequence must both be differentiated from and yet in some way in continuity with the one before. It has at the very least got to be recognizable as belonging to the sequence; but it must also at the very least be distinguishable from its predecessor. Thus the story-teller has to perform a tantalizing balancing act between sameness and difference, in order to make the story happen.

Now we see why every storyteller is a magician and blasphemer, like Salman Rushdie. The storyteller produces the world of becoming out of pure Being, and time out of eternity. Her play of identities and differences breaks up the timeless and unchanging unity of the Self-same to produce the developmental discontinuities that make time thinkable, while at the same time she must hold the time-sequence together by creating illusions of continuity. Continuity through time and change over time are both of them literary artefacts, and they are each other's necessary condition. It is not surprising, then, that the entire world of time and becoming has been disparaged as a magical illusion (maya), and that both in Genesis and in gnosticism/neoplatonism the created world is produced by a series of acts of differentiation.

The storyteller has to get the continuity/discontinuity mix just right in order to please the audience. If there is not enough continuity there will be complaints that the characterization is inconsistent and the story is hard to follow. If there is not enough discontinuity the story will be boring and too predictable, because not enough happens and the characters fail to develop. The really stunning quality of 'narrative drive', which we sometimes find for example in the best Hollywood editing and in early Stravinsky, is achieved by maintaining just the right mix of continuity and discontinuity, and doing so at high velocity and with perfect mastery.

So the storyteller operates in the strange intermediate realm in which we live, suspended between God and pure chaos, between metaphysics and its Other. On the one hand she must conjure up more-or-less stable identities – characters, locations, themes – in order to hold the story together and maintain continuity. Yet on the other hand she must reserve the right to modify any previously-fixed state of affairs, so that she can make the story move forward through time.

By a very strange reversal of our ordinary assumptions, the prime illusion is that of reality, identity, stability. The storyteller is like the continuity-person on a film set who watches over the details of all the shots, trying to ensure that when everything is assembled and presented the illusion of continuity is maintained.

When you make a documentary film, for example, successive shots may have been filmed a year apart. But you must remember to walk into the shot from the correct side, wearing the right clothes, with your hair the right length and with the correct background lighting, weather-conditions and 'atmos' (background sound). The engineers will fix the colour-values afterwards. So identity, reality, stable Being is all a carefully-contrived artefact, a fiction, an illusion! Perhaps this is a clue to the longstanding religious and philosophical denigration of fictions and theatrical presentations: they are too unnervingly truthful. They let the cat out of the bag.

(*ii*) Secondly, this outpouring flow of fictioned identities and differences which gives us temporal succession also gives us time's arrow, its unidirectional character.

We really need that arrow. Human beings seem to begin by supposing time to be circular, an eternal return of the same. Your children, like mine, probably began by supposing that time returns upon itself after a generation. Mine believed that the day would come when they were the parents and we would have become children again. No doubt they looked forward to getting their own back. However, the fact is that we need time's arrow, its unidirectionality, if we are to be able to make moral judgments and if we are to be able to give our lives moral shape. Contrary to what is even yet widely supposed, our life gets all its moral and religious pathos and dignity precisely from the fact that it's a one-way ticket into nothingness. Storytelling, by giving us linear time and moral responsibility, produces life's finality and therefore its seriousness.

(*iii*) Thirdly, sequences also in various ways make time visible, by varying its pace and playing tricks with its scales. Music is in this respect very simple, for we just experience the work at its own pace, allegro or lento. Its tempo becomes our tempo. Film is basically three-layered, for there is the time of the work (that is, the hundred minutes or so of the audience's time that it takes to run through a feature film), there is the time of the action represented within the work, and there is thirdly the director's prodigious freedom to move about in time from shot to shot (jump cut, flashback, slow motion, freeze framing and so on) as he conjures up the illusion of the time of the action within the time of the work.

It is, however, with the novel that playing with time in order to heighten our consciousness of time reaches its very highest degree of complexity. Scaling is very variable: *Ulysses*, operating in close-up, lasts a single day, whereas *First and Last Men* is scaled over millions of years. *Tristram Shandy* is an auto-biography that ends with the author's birth, *Remembrance of Things Past* spends many, many volumes swinging round to recapture a moment from childhood, and *Pincher Martin* recounts a whole life-story and only at the end reveals that it has all been recalled in a drowning man's past moments of consciousness.

Such tricks, as I have said, help make time 'visible' to us. And the queerest, most perplexing fiction that they make visible is the Present. Once a present is established, past and future can be situated in relation to it. But the founding fiction remains that of the Present, and it has a very intricate structure. I define it as the moving intersection of reader-time and narrative-time. Reader-time has a rather narrow bandwidth, being effectively limited to the one or two minutes of short-term memory. Narrative-time, by contrast, has a bandwidth or spotlight that can vary from the twinkling of an eye to donkey's years, and can hop back and forth more or less as it pleases. And my suggestion is that the present of our human life is established in the complicated moving moment of intersection and friction where reader-time engages with narrative-time.

There is no absolute time-scale. Time therefore can only be fixed or realized as an intersection of narratives; for example, when I read a book. There isn't any other way in which a present can be established. For suppose that I lift my nose out of my book, or take my eyes off the screen, to consult a chrono-graph of some kind such as a watch or the sun: I will still need narratives describing how these various chronographs mark time, and how they are to be checked against each other. It follows that just as there is no absolute location, all spatial predicates being relative, so there is no absolute Present, only a present fictioned or fixed (temporarily, dare we say?) where two or more narratives intersect. That is the time of our life, a time that, as I have argued, gets fixed and scaled only with the help of stories.

surprisingly bad image of adults in children's fairytales, for we now have a much clearer idea of what the stories are warning children against, and indeed of why children should react to them with such pleasure and obvious recognition. Yes: to them adults often seem as bad as that. By contrast, consider the behaviour of those who in the late-eighteenth and nineteenth centuries tried to protect the innocence of their daughters by censoring their reading matter. It looks as if they were not doing their daughters a favour, but were merely attempting to keep them weak, ignorant and vulnerable to exploitation. The traditional Puritan concern for the innocence of children and the virtue of women can thus be interpreted as a plot to keep them in subjection by withholding from them the actforms that would enable them to recognize and cope with threats. Everyone who has raised a child must surely know that the more stories it is fed the cleverer and stronger it becomes. And the stories must not be too sweet: if they are to be of any real use to the child, they must be grim and Grimm. In symbolic guise at least, they must confront the child with the realities of sex, violence, misfortune and death. If you have never been shocked by art, you will not be equipped to cope with life.

This argument may establish a presumption against censorship, but it by no means solves all the problems. Indeed, it makes them more acute, for I have rejected the idea that art is distinct from morality and from life. On the contrary, it actually produces both of them. That makes art morally accountable with a vengeance, and I have no doubt that there has to be censorship of some artworks which, by the way they are angled and by the way they influence feelings, strongly incite to serious crimes against the person.

However, we have some more explaining to do. We have not spelled out how a particular sequence of events in a narrative manages to convey a behavioural universal, nor how a behavioural universal gets morally flavoured and becomes a value. There is an interesting and important point here that needs to be studied.

We have a very large vocabulary to describe the various types of narrative: myth, saga, legend, epic, romance, allegory, parable, fairy tale, folktale, anecdote, news, history, fiction, drama, opera, hagiography and biography, as well as such personal narratives as testimony, confession, evidence, memoir, apology and autobiography. A striking feature of these individual testimonies is the way they almost invariably and quite unabashedly confound explanation with exculpation or justification. This strange blending together, especially in first-person narratives, of description with moral plea for the defence is revealed in the ranges of use of words such as 'understanding' and 'account'. By giving an account of my doings I account for myself; and when you understand my account descriptively, you understand morally, that is, by sympathizing. It seems that merely leading you to see my point of view is enough to secure your moral approval of what I have done.

There is a similar blurring-together of narrative recital and moral persuasion in the great public stories. The manner in which history is taught in the nation's schools, for example, is always liable to become a matter of ethnic or political controversy. Evidently people are aware that there is not, and never was, such a thing as scientific or objective history. All narratives communicate values. Very strongly.

How can this be? Consider the clearest case, the apologia. I speak for myself, I tell my story by way of accounting for my conduct. I tell my tale in such a way as to enlist your understanding, your sympathy, your moral agreement. This must mean that my narrative exposes my actforms, and because an actform is a pattern of feeling-flow you recognize my actforms with a certain rush of fellow-feeling. Now you feel/know why I acted as I did, and you are on my side. You are with me. We feel alike. We are as one. I have secured your support.

Evidently actforms are components of narratives and are recognized in the way all words are, by their emotional impact – by the specific feeling-response they evoke. In addition, however, they resemble Plato's forms in functioning not just as universals, but also as standards or norms.

So there are four main elements in the doctrine I am proposing. Like the platonic forms, actforms are both logical *universals* and *values*. But we bring them down into time and the human world by adding that they are embodied in *narratives*, and are recognized by our specific *feeling-responses* to them.

We take the old platonic question first: how is a *universal* somehow able also to function as a *value*? Consider this: the technical scientific description of some particular species of plant or animal is not just a description of any old member of the species, nor even quite of the average member of the species. It is rather a description of a defect-free or 'perfect' specimen of the type. Museums and textbooks will normally exhibit only perfect specimens – which means, specimens all of whose characteristics are general. Many, many specimens are damaged or imperfect, but their deviant characteristics are 'occasional', that is, they are to be accounted for in terms of the unique life-history of that particular individual. For example, my local newspaper recently carried an advertisement saying: 'Lost, £25 reward. Tom cat, one-eyed, torn ear, lame, neutered. Answers to the name of Lucky.' This animal is clearly much valued by its owner, and is doubtless a genuine cat. But it would not win a prize in a cat show. Because of the vicissitudes of its individual life-history, it no longer has all the bits a cat should have.

The standard cat, therefore, has to be a perfect and undamaged cat. No doubt the root metaphor here is that of a template or set-square used by a builder or carpenter. This tool defines the form that the artefact should have. The craftsman uses the tool in first making the object, and may subsequently re-use it to check that the object remains up to standard. Words like *straight, right, upright* and *square* still preserve a memory of the original adoption for moral use of the carpentry metaphor.

Here, as in the cat example, we never made a very sharp fact/value distinction. On the contrary, carpenters and cat-fanciers expect every specimen of the type to be right or perfect, with particular reasons adducible for deviations from the norm where they are found. The same sort of blurring of the fact-value distinction appears in the way we use *example* to mean both any old instance and a morally-standard case. We use *normal* to mean both usual and normative. A *pattern* may be the typical or customary shape of a thing, but it may also be a correct form to be followed. And in Plato's own theory the Form is not only that which all members of the class have in common, but also the perfect and standard-setting case. Every beautiful thing reminds us of and points to the Form of Beauty itself, and the eternal Form of Beauty itself is not only beauty-in-general but also the most beautiful thing of all.

Thus although there is a tradition, going back at least to the scientific revolution, of trying to entrench in our speech-habits a clear distinction between fact and value, is and ought, language itself has somehow managed to go on all this time declining to accept any such clear distinction. It has continued to blur together the average and the ideal, making the general cat the standard-setting, normative cat.

This archaic feature of language is compounded in our modern democratic media culture, where the average very easily becomes a standard that must be lived up to, and where every little movement of signs is a mytheme pushing a value. To take a familiar example, every woman knows that images of women in advertising are not randomly-selected neutral representations of actual females. On the contrary, images of women are images of the powerful cultural norm, Woman. The way the signs move suggests associations, mythemes, values. Have the right looks, buy the right products, make the right faces, and all the right sorts of things will happen to you in all the right places.

In such ways as these, our culture is very highly persuasive and coercive. We are getting messages all the time to the effect that such-and-such, being customary, fashionable and desirable, is therefore obviously also obligatory. Here we go beyond platonism, because for us the standards that govern our lives are not timeless intellectual objects. They have now come down into time; they are cultural. They are embodied in stories, that is, in movements of signs; and these movements of signs condition our feelings to respond to them and move along with them. The world of the mass media is a shifting, manipulated platonic heaven, and our culture thus remains as much steeped in morally-guiding myths as any previous one has been.

We began by saying that in our account of actforms there are four main elements: general or *universal* patterns are presented to us as *normative* via our *feeling-response* to *narratives*. We have argued that still in modern culture, despite all the attempts of scientists and philosophers to establish a clear fact-value distinction, language and other sign-systems continue to present the usual thing as the obligatory thing, the thing that happens to be done as 'the done thing'. And how can this work? Through *narratives*. Although stories may appear to consist of no more than chains of empirical particulars, they are often in practice very powerful models of moral behaviour. We give narratives their power over us by the way we read them. The trick is done by angling, identification and emotion. Narratives make us want to identify and *feel with* the leading characters, female or male, perceiving their world through their eyes and sharing in their value-judgments. We love to do this: we are very ready identifiers, for that is how we learn. Furthermore, the convention is that we do pick up, and are expected to pick up, a behavioural universal from a single telling of a particular story. A fable has a moral; a parable has a meaning.

How does the subtle chain of feelings aroused by a story get imprinted upon us with such general and lasting effect? We need an outline theory. It begins with the fact that the circuitry in the brain is not linear; it is very highly parallelized. Each neuron in the cerebral cortex is wired up not just to one but to hundreds of others, creating an effect like dense crochetwork. A stimulus arising in the cortex may be thought of as spreading across its broad surface like the ripples when a stone drops into a pond, but the circuitry is so prodigiously complex that the halo of excitation generated may have an immense number of different finely-nuanced flavours or feeling-tones, according to the detail of the particular pathways that have been followed on this or that occasion.[1]

For what it is worth, all this corresponds to the subjectively-experienced quality of thought. When we quietly reflect, dream or daydream, we do not think in a logical linear sequence. Thought appears to run semi-autonomously, chains of associated words and symbols radiating outwards in different directions simultaneously. One of them hits something, there is a ping, and the process starts again. So it is indeed as if, one after another, different spreading circles of excitation are set moving and intersecting across the surface of the mind.

It is a common mistake to suppose that we experience our own thought just as it is. Of course we do not: in various ways thought has been demythologized by Ryle, Wittgenstein and others, and de-centred by Freud and Derrida. Thought is not natural but a secondary cultural construction, as is shown by its dependence upon words and other signs. Nevertheless, the analogy between what it seems (in mentalistic language) to feel like to think, and current theory of how the brain works, is of great interest. It points to some such account as the following: thought is set moving (or, the brain is excited) by a perception of difference. Some specific change has occurred, and it activates a neural network. Just one, however, isn't enough. It dies away without leading to anything. The minimum unit of knowledge (equals mytheme or actform or sentence) is the activation of a plurality of neural networks in a particular order. The succession must build up to a small climactic discharge of some kind. This little pleasure-gain sticks: and *that* is an item of knowledge. Unlike the older philosophical tradition, we say knowledge must be grounded in time and in our physiology. Syntax gets the temporal sequence right for the discharge to happen, so that syntax too is physiological. That is why the sentence feels as if it directs a force satisfyingly at a target. For the force to be mustered, built up and discharged the minimum requirement will be the activation of two neural networks. A minimal metonymy. True, there are one-word sentences: but I suggest that in such a case the associations prompted by the word will effectively fill out the force of the sentence. At any rate, there has to be some build-up-and-discharge.

This account shows why it is that the central uses of the word 'story' in our culture are associated with entertainment and the telling of jokes. The after-dinner speaker, the comedian and the television situation-comedy entertain by producing in the audience a continuous succession of small pleasurable discharges of feeling, which are expressed in laughter and applause. If they are to produce any lasting effect upon us, all stories, and not just funny ones, need to entertain us in this way.

The sentences in narratives open up neural pathways, facilitating new sequences of excitation which one day we may have occasion to make use of, perhaps in forming an action of our own, or in interpreting someone else's behaviour. And the run down a new pathway has to be exciting or pleasurable. Note, however, that on the account I am suggesting a narrative does not imprint such a narrow, specific and linear track in the brain as used to be supposed. Rather, I am suggesting that what gets imprinted is something more like a melody or a chain of feelings, which is built up and rounded off. What we remember, and are reminded of, is the emotional flavour or colouring of a previous sequence of excitations which has now been reactivated. Finally, most of the moral directing that narratives do is done by the way we 'place' ourselves in relation to the story as we read, identifying with this character or that.

(b) Stories that have a bad name

The direct moral influence of stories is vividly attested by the extent to which they have a bad name. They must have real power, if they are so dangerous. And a vivid sense of that danger lingered until quite recently. In the 1960s, as a young priest in a northern industrial city, I met two young women whom I knew, hurrying furtively along a back street under big hats. It was evening. Where were they off to? 'The cinema, but we don't want to be seen.' They were members of an evangelical Anglican congregation.

Why the disapproval? Because the cinema was associated with the imagination, the passions, day-dreaming, pleasure, temptation, self-indulgence, the Devil. True belief was rational control and considered speech. You avoided any sort of fantasy. Fiction, from *fingo*, was untruth and sin. It was even idolatry, insofar as graven images were produced by the writer's pen and image-ination. So you shunned them. You accepted God-given reality, and avoided dreaming of anything else. The believer felt like a tram: you were hooked up to the Logos, and power and truth came down from above to rule your life and speech. You zoomed along the track laid down for you, and did not deviate from it.

Reformed Protestantism of that type was platonism expressed

in a biblical vocabulary. Standard Western ideals of rational thought, argument, understanding, knowledge and truth had originally been defined by Greek philosophy in highly anti-narrative terms. The clear understanding of a concept was at one pole of the intellectual world, while story, imagination, rhetoric and poetry were grouped together at the opposite pole. *Logos* was thus the very antithesis of *Muthos*. *Logos* was orderly, direct rational thought and expression. It was lucid, rigorous and dispassionate. It managed to be independent of time and history, for it involved the contemplation of unchanging laws, standards, patterns or Forms. In the English-speaking world people still tend to associate these themes with the 'harder' and more masculine subjects, the natural sciences, logic, mathematics and philosophy, which are seen as being strong, theoretical and relatively unhistorical. By contrast *Muthos* (myth, story) is associated with narrative, poetry and rhetoric, with the imagination, time and human weakness, with ambiguity, persuasion and seduction. In the English-speaking world, which remains under Plato's spell, we associate all this with the supposedly more feminine Arts subjects.

A culture constituted by such a binary distinction between *Logos* and *Muthos* finds it difficult even to frame the question, 'What is a story?' Platonism suggests that it will have to be answered, if it can be answered at all, by finding some general and timeless Form common to all stories. When the form has been discovered, the various particular features of the individual stories can be discarded. Only the Form really counts. Unfortunately, though, stories are extremely diverse, and their most important and interesting features are precisely the features that philosophy disapproves of and tries to abstract away from. A story seduces you into imaginative identification with at least one of its leading characters – but philosophy says you should keep your hand on your ha'penny and not let go of your self-control. Story draws us into a social world, into time, the passions and the interaction of many points of view, and so involves us in a good deal of teasing ambiguity and irony – but philosophy aims to liberate us from all these things. Philosophy believes in clear definition and lucid self-knowledge: it hates the duplicity of literature. The tellers and writers of stories practise various tricks of timing and technique, but philosophy has always prided itself on playing straight, using only argument and not rhetoric. Finally, religious narratives about God and other heavenly beings can only affect us if they picture God and the spirits as having human feelings and intentions, and as acting in an entirely human way. But philosophy since Xenophanes has ridiculed the naive anthropomorphism of religious belief and practice.

So for twenty-five centuries or so there has been a sharp division between two groups. On the one hand the rationalist male clerics – philosophers, monks and also, more recently, the scientists, with their basically Greek ideals of truthfulness, understanding and knowledge. On the other side, the dramatists, poets and other imaginative writers, with at least some female practitioners and in many or most periods a predominantly female audience. For much of the time, if popular idioms are anything to go by, the philosophers have been winning the argument. In common speech stories are very often untruths, *tall stories, whoppers*, self-indulgent *fantasies, fictions* produced by people who are *romancing* and have largely lost touch with reality. Stories are *myths, fairytales, just-so stories, old wives' tales*, idle superstitions, or folktales told merely to terrorize the gullible. It is sheer malice that prompts us to *tell tales* out of school, and to *tell jokes against* respected figures. A typical story-teller is the salesman, seducer or con-artist whose *line, spiel, story* or *patter* is carefully designed to deceive. *Novels, apocryphal* tales and *legends* are a byword for untrustworthiness. *Likely stories* are wish-fulfilments or day-dreams; they embroider the truth, they glamorize or sensationalize reality. And indeed we can scarcely deny that many of the technical skills used by an Alfred Hitchcock to please and divert his audience are precisely the skills of the seducer, the confidence-trickster and the rhetorician.

So story has a dirty name, which is not altogether surprising when for many, many centuries philosophy, religion and science have been hard at work giving it a dirty name.

Yet for most of the same period religious doctrine, the most important truth of all, was expressed in the form of a vast cosmic myth of Creation, Fall and Redemption! Typological and figural exegesis wove the entire Bible into one vast inter-connected symbolic story.[2] Western religious art – sculpture, stained glass, miracle plays, manuscript illuminations – all became highly narrative in style. Western Christianity was allied to Greek philosophy in general and to platonism in particular. At the drop of a hat theologians would reel off the old philosophical criticisms of pagan myths, images and sacrifices. Yet somehow they tacitly exempted their own narratives, images and rituals from the same criticism.

It was all very odd. Philosophy condemned stories for stirring up our emotions and seducing us into identifying ourselves with the central characters. But if this is generally a bad thing, how does it suddenly become a good thing when the central character is St Ursula or Jesus? If stories in general are so temporal, ambiguous and perspectival that they cannot possibly convey eternal truth or even be clearly understood by reason, how can the story of Jesus' life and death be an exception?

To solve the problem, very interesting limits were set to the narrative representation of the Saviour's life in art. Religious thought always wants to exalt the saving, revelatory figure above time and change and make him cosmic. He has ascended to the heavens, and so is portrayed as one absent, like the Jain saint who is merely an empty silhouette cut out of a metal plate. There are well-known examples in early Buddhist, in Islamic and in Christian art of the venerated Founder being represented only by a holy Book, an empty chair, or a pair of footprints. When later the lives of the Buddha and Jesus get to be represented in detail, they are treated as a series of revelatory tableaux, formally-posed still pictures of a moment when eternity broke through and manifested itself in time. The revelation thus did not consist in the horizontal temporal process: in the classical Christian period there were no human-istic lives of Jesus, and painters did not portray a purely human Jesus doing ordinary everyday human things with other people. At least, they did not do this before Rembrandt, for it seemed that the doctrine of the incarnation, by asserting the Divinity of Christ, required that he be dehumanized. Jesus was not imagined, psychologically, as ticking like any other human being. So there was no horizontal revelation *through* the movement of time, but only an instantaneous irruption of the supernatural *into* the temporal sphere. The eternal manifested itself in a symbolically-laden moment when time stood still. Each of these occasions had a formal title, an Old Testament type, a theological significance and a set iconography. It was 'the Adoration of the Magi', 'the Baptism of Christ', 'the Agony in the Garden', or whatever. Almost every surviving pre-1640 painting of a scene from the life of Jesus falls into one or another of these standard highly-theologized and allegorical slots. The life of the Buddha came eventually to be treated in just the same way, for example in the great bas-reliefs at Borobudur. The set-piece revelatory scene was thus viewed as an icon of eternal truth, and only such objects were fit to be set up in places of worship. It was indeed possible to believe in a temporally-ordered succession of 'mighty acts of God' as recited in the Creed and observed through the liturgical year; but because the heavenly world was so sharply distinguished from the human and temporal world, it was not possible to believe in a divine revelation that was fully immanent within the horizontal temporal movement of an ordinary human life. Accordingly nobody thought you could put up in church a non-supernaturalist image of Jesus as an ordinary human being, imagined as if by a novelist. A somewhat ribald treatment of Jesus as an ordinary human does crop up here and there in the mystery drama of the Middle Ages; but this reflects an unofficial and lay point of view. The official Jesus was a Jesus seen in terms of fixed slots, a Jesus taken out of time and humanity and made into a theological allegory. The attempt to write ordinary dialogue for Jesus in a radio play caused public scandal within living memory, and Muhammad cannot yet be portrayed on screen.

To this day suspicion of the fiction-writer and the dramatist lingers in religious circles. The fear is that the imaginative writer's mind will somehow dissolve away the dogmatic truths of faith. Faith can stand up to science, but not to the creative imagination. It is as if not only philosophy but also much of religion were actually constituted on the basis of the repression of fiction, despite the fact that Judaism and Christianity are both very highly narrative faiths. Similarly, modern philosophy successfully distanced itself from any serious consideration of poetry, drama and fiction until the rise of German Idealism.

In our tradition fiction has been almost demonized. The obvious narrative elements within the faith itself were in various ways defictionalized, for example by platonizing allegorical, typological, figural and straightforwardly dogmatic exegesis, and by the 'tableau' iconographical practice to which I have referred. In addition, an impassable barrier was erected which simply prevented people from examining the resemblances between narrative themes in one's own religion and very similar themes in other religions. My beliefs are God-given straightforward Truths: other people's beliefs are demonic parodies, heathen fables, blasphemous fictions or whatever.

The historic demonization of imaginative fiction by philosophy and religion has yet to be fully explained. Our present discussion suggests that faith fiercely repressed the recognition of its own very human narrative and emotional character in order to lend itself supernatural authority and credibility. Supernaturalism was thus always a falsification, and the meaning of religious myth was always straightforwardly human. Only, it did not wish to know its own character. But at least the old demonization of imaginative fiction bore indirect testimony to the formidable power of what was instinctively felt to be an adversary of dogmatic belief. This indicates that the rehabilitation of the literary imagination within philosophy and religion will have great consequences. We will finally give up supernaturalism, dogma and the historic flight of faith from humanity and time. When faith is able to accept the application to Jesus of the fiction-writer's imagination, it will at last begin truly to believe in his humanity – and therefore also in ours. Furthermore, the general appropriation of a fully fictional or human Jesus will humanize the divine more completely than Christianity has yet known.

(c) Stories that satisfy

In what way do stories satisfy? Presumably by meeting a need – even though it be a need that they have themselves created. Stories satisfy, but never satisfy completely. We always want more, so that we become addicted, endlessly pursuing a plenitude of satisfaction that remains always just beyond our reach. When I say that I seek satisfaction, I mean I want my fill, the implication being that hunger is a good basic metaphor for a number of other desires and needs which equally urgently demand to be met. Such needs are often spoken of as devouring. Metaphors of eating, biting and swallowing are readily transferred from the table to the bed, the altar and the study. People bite in lovemaking, eat the Body of Christ, and devour books.

Interestingly, we regard the implied aggression here as being entirely healthy. Certainly it's a sight better than the alternative, which is to be passively eaten up by envy, bitterness or jealousy. The clearest case is that where your honour or reputation have been impugned, or where you have suffered injustice. If that is your plight, then all agree that it is better not to do nothing and risk embitterment, but to take the active line and get out and fight. You should demand satisfaction, struggling to the last breath for redress, justice and the publication of the truth. If you don't fight but brood, then the injury you have suffered will fester and gradually poison your soul. Metaphorically speaking, it seems that the drive for satisfaction is also a drive to purge oneself of something, as well as a drive to devour something.

What do we want to be rid of? Standard idioms suggest a threefold answer. Some form of psychic energy has accumulated to a degree that causes us to feel acute pressure or tension. It threatens to poison us. We want to discharge or expend it, and then we'll feel better. But some impediment seems to be preventing our free expression. We are blocked, constipated or frustrated. So the demand for satisfaction becomes, secondarily, the demand for the removal of a blockage. By a further extension we may go on to suggest that what we need is an 'outlet-form', by which I mean a cleared and prepared channel along which the expression or discharge can learn regularly to route itself.

The notion of satisfaction, on this account (and remember all that we are or can be talking about is the metaphors used in standard linguistic idioms) thus contains three elements: energy needing discharge, the removal of a blockage, and the provision of a channel.

On this sort of account, a story gives us satisfaction in the form of anticipatory pleasure. It shows the way to gain relief. The chain of symbols in the story opens a neural pathway and gives us a preliminary fantasy-gratification. Now we have the channel opened, we'll know what to do next time. By following this particular path or network I'll be able to solve my problem, removing the block, expressing my desire and obtaining gratification.

Stories thus teach us tricks of successful self-management. Through them we learn about our own special tastes and orientations; we learn by experimenting within our imaginations how we can optimize our own life-satisfaction.

In his *Project for a Scientific Psychology* Freud suggests some such account as this, and we drew upon it in the first section of the present chapter.[3] Freud writes as if he is proposing a materialist model of something called 'the mind', which he identifies with the brain. I suggest, more cautiously, that all he can be doing – all that 'thought' can ever be doing – is attempt to systematize metaphors already established in standard linguistic idioms. People certainly do talk as if hunger or sexual desire accumulate within us until we suddenly become aware of them. Then we need to be able to discharge this accumulated tension, or to relieve these pangs. How is this to be done? We need to know what to do to obtain satisfaction or gratification. This knowledge has to take the form of a lot of cut pathways within our brains. Running along these pathways, the energy expends itself in the sequence of behaviours through which it finds satisfaction. The central nervous system thus learns and trains itself to become self-regulating and, as people say, well-adjusted. That means, it works efficiently to keep itself in equilibrium.

To this process stories make a vital contribution: they precut the pathways. In addition they also teach us how to dream, fantasize and simulate for ourselves, so that we can also carry out our own imaginative experiments into possible future courses of action. Thus stories and simulations develop the self. Stories, as people say suspiciously, put ideas into young people's heads, an idiom which uses 'idea' to mean a rehearsal for action, a thought of doing something. Stories are highly suggestive. And once again I insist that Freud's supposedly 'scientific' psychology merely systematizes a lot of everyday metaphors.

At this point, however, we begin to move away from Freud. We move a step beyond his Newtonian balance-of-forces view of the self when we observe that stories do much more than open up neural and behavioural pathways for the relief of our desires. They also actually produce the feelings and desires themselves. They don't just reveal to us what are our tastes and inclinations, but create them. Emotions are constructed in language. Dante's doomed Paolo and Francesca were taught by the romances they read the interesting and delightful secret of how to fall in love, and not merely how to perform intercourse. It is not that we first have definite, structured feelings and desires and only *then* discover that a particular neural network cut by a particular chain of signs opens the one and only behavioural pathway for the successful discharge of this or that emotion, for this doctrine simply faces too many difficulties. Many feelings, like that of being romantically in love, are well-known to be culturally produced; others are too specific to be plausibly thought of as natural; and all feelings in any case need to be carried in words if they are to be identified. You don't first have a feeling and then find the right word for it; on the contrary, the right word brings the feeling. Suppose you are a pregnant woman who in the middle of the night suddenly has one of those odd intense cravings. You simply must have vanilla or black-currant. But how do you know just what it is that you want? Do our desires naturally come as specific as that, even before we put them into words? Obviously not. What has happened in this case is that, as people say, for some reason you've got black-currants on the brain. Childhood associations or something have put the word into your head, and now you have just got to have blackcurrants. The word has brought with it the desire, or if you would prefer a slightly different construction, the word and the desire are so bound up together that when you've got blackcurrants on the brain, the energy with which that particular sign keeps running across your sensibility and writing itself into your daydreams just is your desire for the flavour of blackcurrant. The moving sign is the feeling, and the word produces and forms the desire.

I am saying then that we should not see signs and stories as having been skilfully tailored to fit the shapes of our desires, nor as reporting the discovery of what by trial and error have been found to be efficient technologies for the satisfaction of our desires. Rather, stories actually produce desires and patterns of behaviour. They teach us and equip us with selves to be, feelings to have, actions to perform, people to meet, games to play, and a world to inhabit.

In his *Treatise on Sensations*, the Abbé de Condillac argued that selfhood can be recognized only when some change or difference has arisen within experience.[4] But I am saying we need a bit more than that. We need not just a sign and its difference from other signs; we need also a bit of narrative, for the person is always *dramatis persona*. To be a self I need a role, a part to be playing. Stories supply materials for constructing our roles.

Stories then provide us internally with a functioning economics of selfhood, and externally with a theatrics of the life-world and the various parts that we are going to be playing in it. The self as a self-regulating system is made by stories, and the dramas of everyday life in which it plays its various roles are also scripted by stories. The wisdom of the great scriptural faiths was to understand how profoundly scripted our lives are. And this leads us next to consider the doctrine that stories please and satisfy us insofar as they explain our life and give it meaning.

Old-style Plato-to-Kant philosophy tended to separate reason from the passions. At least, some strands in its argument seemed to be looking for such a separation. But the split could never be completely and consistently carried through, for what sort of personal *life* could the life of an entirely passionless rational soul be, and what could motivate it to seek the intelligible world? Emotion could not be entirely eliminated. The platonic soul had to be driven by a kind of erotic yearning for the heavenly world, and the Kantian moral subject had to be filled with an emotion of reverence for the (purely rational) moral law; and almost the entire tradition between Plato and Kant proposed as the chief End of human life a state of blissful contemplation which could not be conceived of as quite 'apathetic', or passionless. The life of the mind and its final goal must be represented as being in some sense desirable, or how can we commend it? Furthermore, to reach the goal you must strive, battling your way through a series of stages, and this striving requires emotional energy to power it.

If even in the older tradition human reason could therefore never become entirely divorced from the body and the passions, then still more in the newer tradition human rationality needs to be seen as embedded in our language, our social interaction, the play of our feelings and the temporally-extended stories of our lives. Reason needs to be 'aestheticized', brought down into the body, the passions and the life-world. We should not be bullied into accepting that mathematical physics is the standard and primary case of rational discourse. For there are obvious philosophical arguments (we have been giving them) for holding that there is a specially narrative kind of rationality which is logically primary. And this narrative kind of rationality is active, passionate and practical, forming and producing life.

The most influential recent theory of how stories have meaning and tell us about life has been the structuralist theory of myth.[5] It says that stories represent and mediate between the great binary oppositions that frame our lives – nature and culture, the world above and the world below, life and death, male and female, human and animal, and so on. The stories justify, explain and reconcile us to these oppositions, and so on. The presumption is that we experience the great oppositions as puzzling or painful, and the myths as working to produce a mood of acceptance and even resignation.

Our own discussions prompt reservations about this account. As we see it, the myths do not merely accept the great binary contrasts as natural facts to which we need to be reconciled, for in our view the oppositions are themselves produced within narrative. We made them; we can remake them if we do not like them. Neither complaint nor resignation are quite in order. Both postulate too much unalterable 'Nature' out there.

Secondly, the classic structuralist account puts the main emphasis on intellectual oppositions and on reconciliation. But our concern has been with the precise kind of satisfaction that stories may give us, and I wish to suggest that it cuts a little deeper than the structuralist account seems to suggest.

What stories ultimately satisfy is life's hunger for itself, its desire to exist, its desire to be turned on, its desire to be given form and made able to flow. We consume stories most eagerly in infancy and then again in our adolescence, at just the times, that is, when our appetite for life is at its strongest. We want to join the game, and stories form and equip us to do so.

Stories create and produce life, and so satisfy life's paradoxical inchoate yearning to be brought into being.

(d) Stories that produce intelligence

People often talk of intelligence as if it were an innate endowment – a certain speed and accuracy in the wiring in your brain perhaps, that you either have or lack. In fact, however, intelligence is socially created. It is taught by a large number of language games and literary forms that everyone learns.

What's more, intelligence is surprisingly equal, if one judges it by the ability to see the point of a joke, or by the ability to keep one's end up in banter at work, or by the ability to keep a tease, a flirtation or a guessing game going. People are much more on a par than is usually acknowledged, because our most important intellectual capacity – that for language – is generally shared.

Two ancient forms of intelligence-teaching-and-testing story are very familiar from the Bible. There is the riddle, of which many examples are preserved in the Wisdom literature, the Samson-cycle and elsewhere, and there are the sagas about tricksters, cunning and resourceful folk-heroes who live by their wits. Genesis has a number of stories about such figures, including Abraham and Jacob and, among the women, Leah and Tamar. We are intended to admire the guile these characters use in their determination to survive, win their rights or get a child.

Doubtless there are such heroes in every culture, and doubtless too in every culture people watch their children battling enthusiastically to learn the rules of jokes, riddle-telling, puzzle-stories and so on. We speak of people who are fast in repartee as being sharp, smart or quick. Their speed gives us a great kick. It establishes social complicity, and thereby enhances our sense of life.

Sometimes delay is used as a quasi-sexual enhancer. In the mystery thriller and the chase thriller we know that the director is witholding explanation and keeping us in suspense as part of the game. We know there is going to be an explanation, but we are made to wait in anticipation for it. Sometimes the very devices by which the hearer is frustrated are converted, as a kind of reward, into the substance of the joke itself. Try this musical one:

A: Knock, knock.
B: Who's there?
A: Knock, knock.
B: Who's there?
A: Knock, knock.
B: Who's there?
A: Philip Glass.

In the classical detective story we know that we are being given enough for us to solve the story before the author presents us with the solution. This is one of a number of genres in which various kinds of intelligence-sharpening games are played between the author and the reader. Parody, satire and dramatic irony are other examples. Sometimes the reflexivity becomes multiple: we take pleasure in our ability to follow the to-and-fro hall-of-mirrors effect of an exchange like the following Jewish one:

A: Why does a Jew always have to answer a question with a question?
B: (pugnaciously): Look, why *shouldn't* a Jew always answer a question with a question?

It is often suggested that Jewish humour in particular, and perhaps by extension all of humour, is the product of repression, with a hint that it is compensatory. Self-mockingly, the Jewish joke gets a sort of substitute satisfaction to make up for the petty humiliations of real life. There is a closely related theory of intelligence as *ressentiment*, something negative, a means by which those who lack physical power can get their own back.

I argue, however, that the vocabulary of wit and irrepressible, bubbling, effervescent vitality rather suggests an equation of intelligence with the energy of life itself. Intelligence is equivalent to speed on the uptake, which is equivalent to emotional responsiveness and warmth (as opposed to being cold, sluggish and frigid), which is equivalent to abundance of life.

We should repudiate – indeed, we should ridicule – the calculating-machine model of intelligence. On the view I am proposing various literary forms and language games work to produce intelligence as a kind of speed and skill in the playing of a game. One twists and turns, ducks and weaves, knocks the ball back and forth. Intelligence is a social skill, socially possessed insofar as the literary forms, language games and so on that teach it are not purely individual creations but are part of a communal heritage. And the dance of wit is the dance of life itself.

desires are able to find symbolic expression, and that to understand how this works is to have the key to the understanding of
desire, narrative and the dynamics of the self. The way dreams
work while we are asleep is a simple model of the way stories
work in our waking lives. In our purposive behaviour we seek to
express and fulfil our desires by acting out stories of their
fulfilment. But in addition to this use of actforms from stories in
the building of our own personal life-stories, we also look to
stories to please us, turn us on, create wishes, arouse libido,
increase our confidence, allay our anxieties and help us to
confront our fears. That is, in addition to their direct role in
furnishing actforms, our stories, dreams and fantasies work
continuously to produce and maintain the dynamics of the self.
Narratives not only form our actions but also keep the engine of
selfhood turning at times when we are relatively inactive and the
self is not in gear. This explains how dreams and stories can be
said not merely to express wishes, but to fulfil them. For while
we are not in gear the mere movement of signs in the narrative,
keeping the self active, is itself all the life, the pleasure and the
gratification of desire that we long for. Expression *is* fulfilment,
insofar as the movement of the signs in the dream or story is all
the time pulling our desire forth into determinate, living and
moving expression. I live, for the moment, in the fantasy or the
story that is just now running through my head. The movement
of the story is the medium in which selfhood swims – or rather,
it is the medium within which the self presently constitutes itself.

If then we ask why and how the mere motion of signs by itself
is able to be biologically gratifying and releasing, the answer
must be that myth creates. We have always entirely misunder-
stood the phrase 'creation myth'. We have supposed that it
meant merely a picturesque description of a cosmic event that
took place at the very beginning of time. But creation myths are
myths not about 'creation' in that cosmological sense, but about
myth itself and its creative power. It evokes desire, orders
experience and maintains life. That is, the creation myth coincides with itself, for it is a story too, and the most potent story,
the story about the potency of story. The creation myth is
the creative myth of how myth creates, ordering experience,

creating value and shaping life. The creation myth – and almost every human being knows one – is the story that enacts the creative power of stories, the many narratives that are going on in us all the time, and in which we live. Scheherazade, herself a story, tells tales to you non-stop to keep you awake, and thereby saves your life as well as her own.

Freud has a graphic example of the way quite complicated narratives are needed to enable what you might have supposed to be the simplest and most straightforward of biological drives to emerge into expression. In various passages added to *The Interpretation of Dreams* around 1909–1914 he remarks upon the way in which during a single night a whole series of dreams, starting from different angles and employing different symbols, may be needed in order to trigger orgasm during sleep in an adolescent.[3] Through the series of episodes the symbolism becomes gradually more confident, distinct and explicit. Freud quotes Jung on the same phenomenon:

> The final thought in a long series of dream-images contains precisely what the first image had attempted to portray. The censorship keeps the complex at a distance as long as possible by a succession of fresh symbolic screens, displacements, innocent disguises, etc.[4]

There could hardly be any more elemental and simple biological function than orgasm. But we human beings are far from straightforward, for in order to acheive it we must have, seemingly 'within' ourselves and running more-or-less autonomously, all the skills and techniques of a master story-teller. We are not turned on unless we are provoked by indirectness and symbolization. A controlled narrative build-up of some subtlety is needed, merely to produce orgasm. Tricks must be played, disguises assumed and obstacles circumvented. I should not need to add that all this is true, not just of the dream-life of adolescents, but of the waking life of adults, too. Human sexuality is a cultural fiction. It simply doesn't work at all without the help of a prodigious amount of illusion, fantasy and hype. It has to be talked up, narrated into being. Indeed, it is precisely because sex is a social and a narrative construct that the social control of the way human sexuality is represented in art and literature is believed to be possible and is considered so very, very important.

The psychoanalytic discovery of a master storyteller continually at work, and needed to keep the self going and solve its problems, gives rise to an interesting question. Whose cunning is at work here? Is the craft of the inner storyteller the cunning of nature, or that of culture? Because the beguiling storyteller uses language and symbolism, not to mention exceedingly complex and subtle literary techniques, it is clear I think that Scheherazade is a cultural implant. So the self is a literary product, a privatization of culture, made of and by stories.

(b) Transformations

When he came to write his gorgeous poetical compendium of mythology, Ovid chose to give it the title *Metamorphoses*.[5] Why? What led him to suppose that the magical transformation of one thing into another is such a universal phenomenon as to be in effect the common underlying theme of all mythology? I have never seen a fleeing woman turn into a laurel bush, nor have you. Besides, many of the most important myths are about topics such as the creation of the world and the first human beings, the founding of institutions, the setting of standards and the defining of rules. In all these cases, surely, distinctions are drawn, identities are fixed and forms are standardized. The world settles down into a stable order. This is the exact opposite of the metamorphosis-theme, which seems rather to be trying to lead us back into an aboriginal Dreamtime, a world of surreal fantasy in which all identities and boundaries are fluid. So what can Ovid have meant by his title?

Ernst Cassirer's theory of myth offers a first clue.[6] Ovid was a poet and a man of enlightenment. The metamorphoses that he is writing about are ones that go on in the poetic imagination. Cassirer, in his 'philosophy of symbolic forms', combined the Kantian notion that the mind forms experience with the common nineteenth-century doctrine that we are animists who cannot help projecting our own images and our emotions upon the world around us. So myth, embodying our human response to experience, is creative and expressive, poetic and constructive. The mythopoeic imagination is rather like the dreamwork in psychoanalysis. It plays with words and freely turns one thing into another. Consider for example how readily we have always seen human beings in terms of animals and vice versa. Some people are wolves and some are sheep, some are hawks and some are doves. In myths as in dreams, such metaphors are objectified. On Cassirer's account a world is something like a culture's communal objectified dream.

Add a further consideration here: everything on its first appearance must perforce be understood in terms of what is already known. The railway locomotive comes into being as an iron horse, and the car as a horseless carriage. That is to say, our very first and most basic understanding of anything cannot help but view it as a metamorphosis of something else that existed previously – which shows what Ovid meant by his title, for a poet is precisely one who chooses and uses words in that way. Inventing new metaphors, finding new symbolic relationships and thus differentiating the world, poetry itself is the divine power at work in Ovid's book.

If I am right, then the *Metamorphoses* is a metaphor for the transformative and productive power of language. That power is *poiesis*. The poet is one who allows language to be itself, one whose work shows what language is. Poetry shows that nothing is ever seen absolutely and just as it is in itself. Rather, language actually works by endlessly seeing one thing in terms of another. Language is the dance of Shiva: it keeps moving on, forever continuing both to produce and to dissolve all identities.

... Including that of the self. Constituted within language, the self can't help but be like everything else that language produces: insubstantial, metaphorical, transitional. Mysteriously, the self too is something whose identity is always in flux. It is always dying-and-rising, never got hold of, always slipping away. So the magical *Metamorphoses* is the book that is an image of its own reader, a mirror to the mind.

(c) Inside and outside

Children draw a house as a human face, square, with a central doorway representing the mouth. On either side of the door and a little above it, windows represent the eyes, and the roof – especially when it is thatched – is like a head of hair.

The metaphor seems to set up a contrast between a private, interior space of selfhood and the public world outdoors. As a person may sit in her house looking out of the window and watching the world go by, so the self sits inside the body, looking out through the eyes at the external world. A series of important contrasts seem to be founded upon this basic model: the outward and the inward, the objective and the subjective, the public and the private, the open and the enclosed. Furthermore, we have since early times linked all these contrasts with the distinction between appearance and reality, between seductive surface and deep inward moral truth. We look into others' eyes as into deep clear waters, trying to see the soul within. All moral and religious seriousnessness has traditionally been regarded as hidden and private, and located within the depths of subjectivity.[7] The exterior public world was, in our modern jargon, merely 'cosmetic' and superficial. It was like a fairground or a theatre, a scene of pomps and vanities, temptations and deceptions.

This world-view suggests that the human soul may exist in one or another of two states, dispersal and recollection. When you stepped out of the house of selfhood into the common world you became dispersed, not to say dissipated. Your soul was scattered, caught up in the role-play of interpersonal relationships and blown about by the winds of contagious emotion. But when you returned into your house, shut the door and closed the curtains, you recollected yourself and became peaceful. The metaphors associate solitude with calmness and rationality, and company with hysteria and distraction.

On this model the most perfect human society, the Carthusian monastery, is like a village at night. Everyone lives alone, and everyone is indoors with the curtains drawn close and the lights off. Everyone remains awake, quiet and attentive in the darkness.

That is how we should be: good people are introverts. In St Paul's vocabulary, the inner man is the real man.

There is, however a certain conflict here between two distinct interests. The metaphors seem to require the holy inner space of recollected selfhood to be a quite different kind of space from the noisy shallow dissipating space of the social world. The private space of selfhood has got to be a space that only one human person can ever enter. It must be unique, inviolable, subject to its own laws, and opening out into eternity. But obviously, the more highly we thus seek to privilege the inner space of subjectivity, the greater the risk of solipsism and madness. Indeed, when we say of somebody that 'she's living in a world of her own', we imply that she's entered a state where you can no longer distinguish sanity from madness. Her world is so much a world of its own that it is no longer subject to any public criteria. That is dangerous. If we desire both to privilege recollected subjectivity and to fend off the threat of solipsism and madness, we will need to claim that there is some kind of *ratio* or pre-established harmony between what goes on within the self and what goes on out in the common world, and within other selves too. That *ratio* secures sanity. I can never get into your house and you will never enter mine, but I must have some warrant for thinking that there is an analogy between my domestic routine and yours.

It is at this point that we may consider the possibility of using our theory of story to prolong the traditional Western account of subjectivity. Stories recount events in the common public world while at the same time producing private selfhood. As we suggested earlier, the leading edge of the narrative moves forward in time like the slide of a zip fastener continuously interlocking the train of public events that it describes, and the 'domestic routine' of selfhood that it evokes.[8] So when a storyteller relates an anecdote to a group of ten people, the story must surely be producing exactly the *ratio* that we have been looking for. The story itself gives the *ratio* between the common world in which it is enacted, and the various subjectivities which in the telling it produces. We all of us know we are in tune with each other and our world insofar as we have stories in common.

Thus a culture's stock of stories, and especially its religious stories, may be seen as actually creating a community of harmonized selves and their common world.

Very well: I am not repudiating this account. But the theory of stories that we are proposing cannot be read as coming anywhere near to justifying the traditional ontology of selfhood. On our account selfhood is not anything deep. There is no depth. Cut me open, and you'll bring to the surface nothing but bones, flesh, and brains. There are no meanings, and there is no self, deep down inside me. Nothing either intelligible or individuating is to be found below the body-surface. The real me is all on the surface and all public. Culture, which individuates and creates intelligibility, is strictly superficial. For it is only on the surface of my body that language moves, emotions visibly flicker, clothes and facial expressions signal, roles are played and meanings can be read. Don Cupitt, the individual as such, is only surface. I have no inside. What you see is all there is: necessarily, the readable has got to be superficial. A book is a lot of two-dimensional surface, and if you can read me like a book, as no doubt you can, then I too must be all surface. Only surface *can* be read. The traditional distinctions between outside and inside, surface and depth must be only metaphorical. They boil down to such differences as those between my own reading of my own surface and other people's readings of it, between a quick guess and a more considered interpretation, and so on. There isn't *really* any depth, for 'depth' is only another metaphor, and as such is itself also on the surface. So there is no literal and non-metaphorical 'inwardness', and the entire rhetoric of subjectivity was only a construct, a figment that guided a now-obsolete form of spirituality. Supposing that there was really such a thing as depth or reality beneath the surface was a mistake like supposing that someone who reads between the lines really is finding something decipherable actually between the rows of printed characters. But there isn't really anything between the lines. Reading between the lines is merely a metaphor for a certain exegetical skill at reading what is given in the lines. Somebody who can read between the lines can pick up delicate hints and ironies. And similarly the self is not something deep, extra, and outside the world of signs. It is merely a kind of literary effect produced by the characteristic way signs, meanings and feelings play upon my surface. Anyone can read me. Admittedly, not all of me gets read. Some of what moves on my surface never gets read by me, and some of my surface folds back on itself like a Moebius strip in self-consciousness, soliloquy and dreams. Nevertheless, I insist that there is only one surface, of which different areas get read in different ways. My destiny is communication. I am fully interwoven with, and am continually passing out into, the common human world. That is why my life should be and is a life of self-giving and dispersal, and not a life of solitary egoistic recollection. I am passing away all the time.

What happens then when a group of us see a film or otherwise hear a story? The distinction between the common world, selves generally, and some one particular self still remains. For there remains a distinction between a chain of signs, its power to evoke upon anyone's surface a play of feelings, fantasies and associations, and the particular way it resounds upon me. And when a group of people hear the same story one can understand both that each person hears it a little differently, and that the story in its enactment makes of them a community insofar as it produces in them some shared patterns of feeling and shared actforms, and therefore the beginnings at least of a common life.

Notice that this theory makes religion intelligible, but at the price of returning it into its own narratives. It proves the humanity of religion. Religion is a set of stories that in the telling produce a society of emotionally-attuned and evaluatively-attuned selves, differentiated from each other, but sharing a family likeness and able to live a common life together. Every society needs a religion, in the sense of a collection of communally-possessed life-guiding stories. But such an account of religion explains and naturalizes it, and we recognize that there is nothing to stop us from inventing fresh stories, or even redesigning religion altogether. Yes: why not?

(d) Simulations, dissimulations.

It is characteristic of the culture of Romanticism, and still more of our own postmodern media world, that the human self lives and moves in a continuous daydream, a flux of stories. Many of these fantasies, simulations and imaginings are generated internally. Others are provided by the various media whose output the average person absorbs for several hours every day.

By historical standards at least, we are immersed in fictions. The self has become extremely pluri-personal, theatrical, a collection of roles. In the practice of life we step from one role to another almost unthinkingly, putting on the appropriate face without any difficulty. Each of us now has the rather labile selfhood of an actor.[9]

In the past things were very different. Over two millennia and more, ascetical and rationalist ideals dominated the culture. In religion as well as in philosophy, the aim was to be lucid, master of your self and guided only by the Truth. Religion typically privileged one set of stories only and sought either to banish, or at the very least drastically to restrict the moral influence of, all stories outside the sacred corpus. As for the sacred stories, they were not really stories at all: they were just the Truth.

From its earliest days Christianity in particular was very hostile both to pagan mythology and to the theatre. The typical psychology of a playactor represented exactly what the Christian was in flight from. Of course the first Christian ascetics who went to the desert and strove to master their own thoughts soon became aware of the activity of the inner story-teller that spins tales all the time inside our heads. But whereas I have called it Scheherazade and have argued that it works to maintain selfhood, they simply called it Satan and battled against it. For us, listening to Scheherazade is a method of self-discovery. We need to listen carefully, for the way we find ourselves responding to her tales shows us who and what we are. For the classical Christian attitude to her, study the Temptation of St Anthony in Christian art. She was a siren, a threat.

Broadly speaking, Christian thought has equated paganism

with a lax proliferation of seductive stories, which tend to disperse the self and make it too plural. The holier your life the harder you tried to restrict yourself to biblical actforms and to silence Scheherazade. You sought to become a unified self, living by one story only.

This, however, will only work insofar as theology can convincingly systematize into one great master-narrative the larte and diverse corpus of material to be found in the Bible and Christian doctrine. The first great attempt to produce such a mighty epic story seems to have been made by St Paul in the Epistle to the Romans, and the last was made by Karl Barth. Between them lived Irenaeus, Augustine, Dante, Calvin and many others. Since both the self and the world are produced within language, the great theological epic was potent enough to generate a unified cosmology and a unified selfhood. The self, the Book and the universe were all of the same shape – and it was a *narrative* shape, the epic of the fulfilment of God's creative and redemptive purpose in each self and in all the world. This story finally broke down only as recently as the 1960s, and present-day fundamentalism represents a last frantic doomed attempt to reinstate it. Fail it must, however, in the modern media-culture and the modern economy. You cannot hope effectively to control the flood of stories, or to systematize them all into one great master-narrative, or to silence Scheherazade. We are stuck now with our plural theatrical selves, our ceaseless tale-spinning and our role-play.

We can still be religious. The Romantic-postmodern self emerges greedy for stories, formed within stories, guided by stories and modelling itself upon characters in stories; and religion, after all, still has the best stories. The stories of religion remain familiar to everyone, and nothing stops us from incorporating them into our lifestyles. I do. Whatever they say, I am a Christian. I live by the Christian stories (though in all honesty I have to add, amongst others). But modern faith is unavoidably a lifestyle, fictionalist, slightly *camp*, affected. The role of 'practising Christian' is now a character part, not a leading role any more. Haven't you noticed? In the past various devices privileged one complex of stories and gave it the very highest social authority. This was 'Truth', humankind's grandest fiction of all. The great master-narrative (i.e., the Bible as read by Augustine, Calvin, etc.) produced a certain psycho-drama in the self, and also a certain meaningful narrative order of things in the world. There was a kind of harmony or structural isomorphism between these two. So the self's life-story, the text of the Bible and the unfolding cosmic plan of salvation were all the same sort of shape. The Book had the power to make your life-story a miniature epitome of the whole of cosmic history. You had had your Genesis, you had lived under the Law, you had received Christ, you were now heading for final glory. You were thus a microcosm, and set at the very centre of things. That was Truth. I knew it once. But since then stories have multiplied uncontrollably. Selves and worlds are all optional. There are many possible small-t truths. In adopting one to live by, we are choosing a life-style. We are choosing a fiction, a story to live by that suits us. We are modish and ironical, a little affected indeed, but it cannot be helped. Everything is on the surface now. There is only a shimmering vibrating surface, across which stories run endlessly. Are we happy to express ourselves and our faith under these conditions? I gulp and I say, 'Yes, I am'. We've no choice left but to accept a world in which everything is optional. Got that?

(e) Feelings and meanings

I have a weakness for Elizabeth Barrett Browning, perhaps because she lived at a time when the politics of heterosexuality was less fraught than it is nowadays. She could write love poetry without feeling that perhaps she was letting the side down. However that may be, the first line of one of her *Sonnets from the Portuguese* just came into my head:

How do I love thee? Let me count the ways.

How does it go on? I can't remember, but as happens in these cases I know I'll recognize it when I come across it. I can feel its flavour already. I can even pick up a faint sense of scandal and heightened excitement, because I feel that she borrows some kind of bold religious metaphor.

It seems that I can remember and identify a delicate sequence of feelings upheld by the rather strong rhythm of the verse in those lines, but the precise words in which those feelings are coded and fixed still escape me. They'll come soon. Meanwhile I have learnt something: thoughts are very finely nuanced chains of feeling, ripples over the cortex that have been fixed in language, and we seem to get at them from the underside. That is, I recover my memory of EBB's words *via* their specific feeling-tone. I feel the melody first, and then after some hesitation the melody brings back the precise words that make up that particular tune:

I love thee to the depth and breadth and height
My soul can reach ...[10]

Thus so far as subjective experience is concerned, feeling seems to precede meaning and to be the gateway to it. Biology appears to concur. We can imagine how in the aroused brain waves of excitation spread out over the neural networks. Brain activity is first felt in consciousness as spreading and shimmering emotion. Somewhere in all those ripples I can sense the presence of the right sequence, already firing, but still on the margins of consciousness. Now we wait for the language generator to come up with the right form of words. Then there is a subjectively-felt click, from which we can tell we've got it right.

From the point of view both of biology and of subjective experience, then, feeling seems to precede meaning, and knowledge works somewhat as follows. Every item of knowledge is coded in the brain as a large and complex pattern of facilitated connections between neurons, the whole forming a great spreading net. Excitation spreads out across the net and is felt subjectively as a distinctive sequence of feelings, rather like a melody. The language-generator converts feeling-melodies into physical sentences. It fits book to lyrics. When I got EBB's words right they reinforced the original feeling, creating the sense of recognition.

On this account all our knowledge is skill-like, and within the brain is grounded in temporal melody-like sequences of biological feelings. I don't want to postulate intelligible inner thoughts. The brain knows only waves of excitation. My mind is entirely on the surface, because intelligibility starts in the motor nerves that produce speech and in a kind of fluttering that occurs in the soft palate, and it ends in the ear. Thus consciousness is strictly superficial. There used to be a phrase, 'a conscious look', which clearly implied the visibility of consciousness. People's facial expressions are their thoughts, and are easily read. We would be less muddled about all these issues if we stopped thinking of the mind as being inside the brain. No, the brain is just biology. The cultural, intelligible you, your mind, is your outer surface. You see and hear and read what's outside your body, and your speech is a motion on the skin of your body. So there is no need for you to think of yourself as having a mind inside your head. Instead I am asking you to bring your mind forward, so that you locate it on your face, in your field of vision, in your speech and in your ears, where all the meaning is. You think out in front.

That being so, we may be ready to grasp the sense in which, from the point of view of philosophy, meaning precedes feeling.[11] The cultural, public world of human communication is logically prior to the shadowy and secondary inner world of biological feeling that it conjures up. We don't have any direct and primary access to the inner world of our own brains. Self-consciousness is produced within the public realm and by language. It depends on things like being able to handle the indexical pronouns, and wondering how we appear in the eyes of others. It depends upon our awareness of our own bodies. So self-consciousness is, as it were, your face. It is all on the surface. You are not self-conscious deep inside. 'Deep inside' there is only the brain. You are self-conscious on your skin. It is the self-conscious public-language realm which comes first, and *via* which alone you can construct some sort of account of your inner world of the brain and its shadowy biological feelings. Only language can create consciousness, so only language can flash a lamp backwards into your brain to make you dimly aware of your biological feelings. We need public help in order to look back into the private world. We start with language, and then work back to the cerebral cortex and the ripples of excitation spreading over the neural nets.

We can now descry the sense in which a human being is entirely culturally-formed, and made of stories all the way through. We can gain access to our brains and our biological feelings only through language. But in language our feelings are already represented as ordered into 'melodies' – meaningful sequences, or sentence-shapes. And the sentence-form is already narrative and expressive. So a human being can live only within an order of meanings; that is, a human being is always already busy constructing life as a story. That is why in early works of fiction like the *Thousand and One Nights* or *Gil Blas* characters introduce and identify themselves by relating their histories. I am the story I can tell about my own life, and the more artistically coherent and ethically satisfactory the story I can tell the more emotionally fulfilled I shall feel.

The stories we can tell about our own lives have various subplots and loose ends. They are constantly threatening to break down or become incoherent. We have to keep on improvising, stitching and patching, amending our histories. We are indeed like Scheherazade, who told tales to keep her life going. One of the reasons why we love fictions so much is that we *need* them so much. We want to borrow bits from them for use in building our own greatest fictional works – our life-stories.

(f) Stories and explanations

I can understand nothing unless I understand something of how people tick, what their purposes are and why they act as they do. The proof of this is simple: I can't understand anything until I can understand language, and I can't understand language unless when someone speaks to me I can pick up the drift, the force or the point of what she's saying. I've got to grasp what her game is, how she expects me to take what she's saying and what range of possible responses I have to choose from. Utterances are also actions, are indeed the most delicately angled of all actions. We need to be able to tell where the speaker's coming from. Otherwise we may entirely fail to get the message.

To understand language, we must be able to grasp what game is being played and what the point of the game is. I have to take on board not just what the other speaker says, but what she's getting at, what she is trying to accomplish in speaking as she does. And that in turn means that in order to work out what she's up to I have to invent a conjectural story about what her purpose is, and how she sees the present exchange being so managed (by her) as to contribute to the fulfilment of that purpose. And do I for my part want to go along with all this; or if I resist, shall I do it by pretending incomprehension, by overt opposition, by teasing, by bargaining or by some form of deviousness or obliquity? Whichever of these lines of response I choose, she'll then be put in the position of having to read me – and so the battle will go on.

I am saying then that I can understand nothing unless I can understand how people tick. That is, I must understand the extraordinarily complex ways in which they organize chains of actions, linguistic and other, in order to fulfil their purposes. And I must also be able to grasp the manifold ways in which people may cooperate with, manipulate or frustrate each other.

For this I shall need large numbers of illustrative stories explaining human actions and interactions on at least four levels: what people's desires and purposes are, how through strings of actions they may set about fulfilling these aims, the 'secrets of the human heart', that is, the various ways in which people may conceal or be unaware of their true aims, and the dramatics of human interaction.

When I have got it, my story-library will be of great value to me as a source of interpretative rules and narrative hypotheses. Suppose for example that something my friend has just said has puzzled me. I cast about for a recollection of something analogous. I find something. It gives me a clue. The clue suggests a rule of the form: 'Someone like her, saying such a thing in such circumstances, probably has such and such an intention in mind.' I thus frame a narrative hypothesis about what she's up to. What I next say needs to be so angled as to fish for a little corroboration of my hypothesis.

Listen carefully to good dialogue – especially between men

and women. You will notice that to a quite extraordinary degree people choose not to give a straight answer to what has been asked or said. Instead they react to what they suspect may have been intended by the last remark. It is as if every conversation were really a contest of narrative hypotheses, a conflict of stories about what each of us thinks he's up to and suspects the other of being up to, and, yes, a struggle for the moral advantage.

I have been trying to suggest that all our knowledge and understanding are inescapably temporal, and therefore inevitably keep dropping into the narrative mode. Now we make the point more strongly: in all the relationships, utterances and activities of life we are attempting to find, and perhaps also to act upon, a morally satisfying story about what is going on. We never quite reach this goal towards which we are oriented. In the meanwhile, talk about cognitive need, about the meaning of life and about the human quest for meaning expresses our perennial yearning for a master story, a story that will really *stick* and make enduring moral sense of life. In the daily business of life ignorant armies of stories about people's intentions, real and imputed, clash by night. Everything is tangled and obscure. Why are we always at odds with each other; why is mutual understanding so hard to maintain? It seems to me that nothing adds up. People never really communicate. They merely wrestle, without ever quite understanding what they are wrestling about. What could be more overwhelmingly desirable than a single grand public guiding and reconciling story, with a part ready-scripted for each of us and a plot understood by all? If we really had such a story, perhaps we would be at peace with each other and with life.

Undoubtedly we expect such a story to promise us that life will have a *denouement*. We often demand to be reassured in the closing pages that all the loose ends will be tied up, the whole truth will come out and justice will be done. Even today, much or most of imaginative literature remains highly 'theological', insofar as it still by implication makes some such promise to the reader. By its very form a book seems to promise to give satisfaction, a happy ending, a resolution of the story. If it fails to keep such an implied promise it is described as 'black', *noir* in the technical sense, and not much literature is black. *Film noir* remains perhaps the only widely popular 'black' art. By contrast most literary genres, and especially the classical detective story and the courtroom drama, are thoroughly theological. The main concession to modernity is that much of the work of upholding the moral order is allocated not to God but to the human central figure, who uses scientific reasoning, literary imagination in constructing narrative hypotheses, and a great deal of moral courage and persistence to ensure that in the end innocence gets vindicated and guilt exposed. The reader is supposed to join in the action and, as it were, to contribute to the solution. Thus even where the text itself is designedly left open, we will tend to close it by the way we read it. But notice that in these literary genres the human pursuit of justice is rarely presented as an illusory or vain endeavour. On the contrary, even if the authorities are corrupt and the social order is unjust, we are still in a world where there are clear moral distinctions, and plenty of evidence is available to the persistent and honest enquirer. Moral truth is out there waiting to be found and published. Writer, hero and reader are all moral realists, in the sense that for the purposes of the book it is agreed by all three of them that there is only one objectively true morality. It is built into the book. We know what it is. Those who flout it cannot avoid leaving traces. Picking up these clues, we can help to ensure that justice gets done, which is what all the good people (the vast majority of us, of course) want to see happen. We are expecting to see all the loose ends neatly tied up in a single correct solution to life's riddle, and we are not disappointed.

All this is very highly theological, but a little ironically or self-mockingly so, because the book or film is confessedly genre fiction and therefore only a game played according to well-understood rules. Whatever the disappointments of real life, art at least can continue to offer a world in which wrongdoers are identifiable and can be punished. That is what we want, so that is what we are given: the moral order as a myth and a game. In this way the crime writer, the Western film director, and the rest of them please us by restoring as ironical fiction what has been lost as dogmatic faith.

This gives us a hint. Genre entertainment shows that theological ways of thinking, when given an ironical twist, remain immensely popular. Is it possible that we might be able to formulate a quite-deliberately ironical and fictionalist theology, which might nevertheless be capable of inspiring moral endeavour? You think I'm joking? Wait and see.

(g) Life stories

We remarked earlier that in the picaresque novel characters who appear on the scene for the first time introduce themselves to the reader by relating their life-histories. This fills us in on where they have come from, how we may expect them to behave and what sort of people they are. The character is in effect saying: 'Listen to my story. It's me, it's my message for mankind. It is my piece, what I have to say. It is the storyline that has run through my life. This storyline identifies me. It is the meaning my life has had, and the lesson it has to teach both to me and to others. Everyone has some such story: it is what they are, and what they have to say.'

This lesson that my life so far has taught me is its 'moral', in the sense of a proverb or a bit of practical wisdom about life. So close is the link between story and moral that when a modern person exclaims ruefully, 'That's the story of my life!', we may take it that she means: 'I too have repeatedly suffered similar frustrations, misfortunes and disappointments; I too have learnt how wide is the gulf between initial hopes and eventual out-turn!' The story is in effect equated with the moral lesson about life that it teaches. The story we have to tell is the sobering piece of advice we have to give. The picaresque character's autobiography similarly invites us to consider how odd and unpredictable people's fates in life are. What a strange con-catenation of misfortunes brought this one to his present plight, and contrariwise, how unexpected and curious that one's good fortune! We are invited to marvel at the incomprehensible variety of life in a rather special mood, neither moralistic nor pessimistic. That is, we certainly cannot detect any orderly moral providence at work in life, tidily ensuring that in the end

the good people prosper and the bad ones suffer. But nor are
we led to a Thomas Hardy type of moral pessimism. Instead we
are filled with a kind of pleasurable astonishment at life's
unaccountable ups and downs. Certainly human beings are at
the mercy of fortune, but there is good fortune as well as ill
and human beings are great survivors. Besides, what is the
alternative? In our world we are the playthings of fate and
ignorant of our own futures, which at any rate means that there
is always hope for a change of fortune. Consider the other
possibility, a morally tidy predestinarian world, neatly divided
into one group of people with every reason to be self-righteous
bigots and a second group of people with every reason to
consider themselves damned souls. Would that really be a better
world? At least, in the world we have got, arrogance is sometimes brought low and lowliness is sometimes raised up. Both of
these events are good to see, because the accidental sort of
justice we call 'poetic' is the only entirely pleasing kind of
justice. As for human justice, it stinks. You know that. It always
did and it always will.

Picaresque seems to flourish as a popular lowlife genre in
morally disciplinarian societies. Artists like it for its immoral
moral, for its moral is that our amoral universe is a whole lot
less immoral than a more moral world would be. Furthermore,
it is in precisely such a variegated and morally unpredictable
world as this that art can flourish and life can be loved for its
infinite generous absurdity.

The agreeably paradoxical suggestion that moral scepticism is
morally greatly preferable to morality can be taken a stage
further by comparing the picaresque autobiography with two
other types of story of one's own life. I'll call them the success-
story and the apology.

The success-story is usually written late in life as an example
to a much younger generation. It urges the reader to share the
author's lowly origins, his indifferent success at school and the
struggles of his early life. All the way through the writer is
implicitly urging the reader: 'Follow my course, if you want to
end up being as fine a fellow as I am!'

The apology is typically produced by someone who is under

attack: a politician, a controversial public figure, a defendant on trial. We listen because we find the perspectival character of truth interesting. We want to hear her side of the argument, her story. In this case we use the word story to signify what we know will be a consciously-partial account, the case for the defence. The story is going to be told in such a way as to enlist the reader's support. Indeed, it is the apologist's positive *duty* to make the strongest and most plausible case on her own behalf that she can.

In very different ways, both the success-story and the apology want the reader to identify and sympathize with the hero of the story that is told. It is hoped that we will admire and try to imitate the successful person, and that we will give our sympathy and support to the apologist. Both are moralistic; both invoke the idea of (in a broad sense) compassion. I mean simply that the narrator tries to secure the moral involvement of the reader. By contrast, the picaresque autobiography is in no way tendentious and imposes a much lesser moral demand upon the reader. When we have read some unfortunate's account we may be sobered, we may recognize that life is like that, we may be filled with wonder at the misfortunes she has suffered. But the direct moral identification of reader with storyteller is scarcely sought at all. We are buttonholed and asked to listen, and that is all. There is certainly no suggestion that this catalogue of misfortunes amounts to a model for imitation. The storyteller is not saying, 'Live like me', but only, 'Listen to what has happened to me'. Nor does the story leave us particularly inclined to wax indignant at the injustice of life, because for reasons already mentioned we are not at all sure what it would be like for life to be just or whether we even want life to be entirely just. In the picaresque novel when a story has been told the other characters usually react good-humouredly, philosophically and with perhaps a certain rough human fellow-feeling – but not with intense moralistic compassion or indignation, because it does little good either to pretend that life is just or to expect it to be so.

The apologist's life-story is acknowledged to be self-serving; that is its function. The success-story is unconsciously self-serving, a display of naive self-satisfaction. But the picaresque autobiography is almost always presented to the other characters and to the reader as being simply the unvarnished truth. We find no reason to doubt the story we hear. Yes, this is how life really is: unpredictable, gloriously absurd, and to be taken as it comes. When fortune happens to be favouring us we should neither congratulate ourselves too much nor expect too much in the way of love and admiration from others. When we are cast down, there is no point either in complaining too loudly, or in expecting too much by way of compassion from others. The true heroism is to have survived without being too much damaged, either by good fortune or by ill.

In different periods people are identified in rather different ways. Sex, age and place in society are always important, but by themselves these indices are not sufficient to identify just one individual. What else is there to add? In the Middle Ages there was above all your relation to the virtues and vices, the great moral universals under which every one of your actions fell. So people were identified as miserly or courageous or whatever. The individual was one who exemplified a moral universal. But in picaresque, people are individuated by their life-histories. No doubt all life-histories are in a sense absurd, and all teach the same lesson about life's unpredictable reverses of fortune; but at least each person's catalogue of misfortunes and disappointments is different and her own. I am the list of my own mischances, I am my own weird and wondrous fate.

Neither in the mediaeval world nor in the picaresque is there much recognition of the unique individual personality. If Chaucer is exceptional in this respect, then he is the sort of exception that – as they say – 'proves the rule'. Other writers seem not to have the vocabulary or the technical resources. The contingent particular as such is not highly valued. In the Middle Ages all value resides in the universal, and the particular is assessed only in terms of its relation to the universal that it exemplifies. In picaresque the individual is unique, but her uniqueness is not a valuable uniqueness of her own character and personality. On the contrary, we get surprisingly little sense of such things. In the picaresque our uniqueness is grounded in absurdity, being given to us willy-nilly by the extraneous absurdity of life. I am the unique absurdity of my own fate, and you of yours.

Gradually during the Enlightenment, however, the universal recedes, making it possible for writers to ascribe more value to temporal particulars and to the processes of personal growth and development. The change is slow and irregular. Writers as diverse as Molière, Bunyan and William Law[12] can continue to be very shrewd and entertaining while still for the most part working with the old moralistic and emblematic categories. Other writers, however, such as Hobbes, Spinoza and Hume, are already declaring that if we are to make any progress in understanding psychology, we must begin to look at our fellow-humans naturalistically and not moralistically. Hume is one of the first thoroughly secular historians. He so tells his historical story as to show how the nation, a complex individual, has over time evolved its own distinctive character and institutions. A unique and valuable individual thus emerges from a purely contingent history. Since Hume himself draws an analogy between an individual and a nation,[13] he might in principle have gone on to examine how out of the purely contingent details of a person's life-history a unique and valuable personality is formed. But he does not take this step, no doubt because he always remained too much the philosopher.

What does this mean, that Hume remained too much the philosopher? It means that even though he was a sceptic, he was still an unmarried male contemplative like virtually every other philosopher from Plato to Kant. He still felt the need to look for philosophical happiness in the same direction as all his predecessors had done, namely towards a timeless and universal objective order of Reason. This order of Reason had always been a kind of exalted, spiritualized and generalized masculinity, 'phallogocentrism'. Not, I hasten to add, that Hume himself was any kind of monk or rationalist ascetic: a stout fellow in every sense, he was worldly and loved company. He was indeed losing belief in the old objective order of Reason. In his thinking it had become reduced to a mere set of empty tautologies. The philosopher was a sceptic, who regarded with resignation and detachment the greatness of Nature and the littleness of humanity. Hume was so far from any belief in an eternal order that he regarded knowledge and morality as reducible in the end to mere customary patterns of feeling; but as he so often says, he still needed a tincture of old-style intellectual contemplation to be for him an alternative to religious faith. For consolation, then, he looks towards the old order of Reason, even though it is now vacant. So he remains a philosopher, and does not quite make the turn to subjectivity and to personality. That was left to writers who were in no way committed to the old philosophical order – poets, literary Romantics, women writers.

For these people, the authors of biographies, *Bildungsromane*, romantic fictions, autobiographical poetry and so on, the self is an organism that grows and develops through time. But whereas biological organisms merely exemplify universals (every cat being just a typical cat), each human self progressively individuates itself by its action in, and its response to, the contingent details of its own life-story. Each person's life-task is to become a unique individual.

What we are describing here is not the same as 'the birth of Man'. In Foucault's account of this latter event, for example, the Enlightenment recentred the culture upon the finite human subject. 'Man' believed himself capable of objective knowledge of the world, moral and political autonomy, progressive social reform and (in due course) technical world-mastery. But all this, important though it doubtless was in its day, was still a highly masculinist programme, with its dreams of godlike knowledge, power and blessedness. It was a humanism that put 'Man' – i.e., self-affirming, self-possessed and masculine man – in the place of God. But our present concern is with something rather different, the production in Romantic and post-romantic culture of a ceaseless flood of stories of the formation of selfhood which continues to the present day. This material is not especially concerned with public life, politics and technology. It is about private life, subjectivity, the passions and personal ideals. It is about the world of women and children, family relationships, young people entering adulthood, courtship and marriage. Following Goethe, it is about the individual's personal growth towards maturity, harmony and stability. The name of the central character whose development we are following very often figures in the title of the work. Often she's a worthy young soul, a little plain and blank, which makes it easier for the reader to identify with her. She has been precipitated into a slightly better class of society than she is accustomed to, but her virtues will attract notice and she will end by making a good marriage. She will become someone (and the book prudently ends before we have had time to reflect that she's going to become, poor thing, someone eminently forgettable).

For nearly two centuries now we have lived surrounded by such fictions. They are quasi-religious works, a bourgeois humanist recycling of the old theme of the progress of the soul. Our world has now become so complex and fast-changing that people can no longer live lives that are governed by stable customs and religious imperatives. The body of stories that people live by cannot be held within a single fixed canon. Instead we have now a whole living literature which is being continuously added to and modified as values change.

The message, though, remains as theological as ever. It is that despite all appearances to the contrary our life is not entirely chaotic. It can become meaningful. There is a Telos, a goal for us, so that our life can be a story that develops and gets somewhere. Practise our heroine's virtues, keep to her standards, and you can win through to happiness and social acceptance. Do not doubt that you too can become one of those who have made it.

Stories are and remain theological in a fourfold sense. Every story just by being a story constitutes a promise that life can be meaningful. That is the job of stories; they make life make sense. Secondly, every story has, is and conveys a moral in the sense of a piece of practical wisdom about life. The man in the tavern who tells you his story is telling you what life has taught him. We all have at least one message that we want to give to our fellow humans – our own story. Thirdly, every story inculcates values: it is strongly action-guiding or regulative. Stories teach people by what values they should live. Finally, stories in the telling define the identities of their own leading characters. Although art tries to maintain a certain openness, every story cannot help but become something of a closed text. The leading figure just is what we take the text to represent him as doing, saying, undergoing and becoming. The text makes him emblematic, for as we have seen there is a curiously intimate link between storyline, moral and identity.

4

HISTORIES AND MYTHS

(a) Truth as fiction

People are not very good at remembering unconnected items. There is a memory-testing game in which a tray laden with miscellaneous bits and pieces is put in front of the competitors for ten or twenty seconds. It is then whisked away, and they have to write down a list of as many of the objects as they can remember. It is surprisingly difficult to manage more than eight or so, unless one resorts to some kind of *aide-memoire*.

How then can we improve our memories? Many people begin by attempting to make a kind of mental photograph of the scene, keeping still, concentrating and staring hard. Then in retrospect they try to recall the picture in detail. This does not work very well. You do a little better if you restrict yourself to a fixed list of items that you remember in sequence, as codified religion does with its seven deadly sins, ten commandments and twelve apostles. Better again is to arrange a number of the items in rhythmic, scanning doggerel verse like 'Thirty days hath September, April, June and November ...', a formula which works so well that with its help almost everyone in Britain remembers how many days there are in the month.

Many of the most popular mnemonic devices are incongruous sentences. The thread of syntax running through them makes the words easy to recall. The first letter of each word is the same as the first letter of the corresponding word on the list to be remembered. Thus 'Some *m*en *h*ate *e*ating oranges' yields the names of the great American Lakes: Superior, Michigan, Huron, Eyrie, Ontario. 'Richard of York gave battle in vain' encodes the colours of the spectrum: Red, orange, yellow, green, blue, *i*ndigo, *v*iolet. Similar devices are used in mathematics: 'Some officers *h*ave *c*urly *a*uburn *h*air *t*o Oppose *a*uthority' summarizes the trigonometric identities: *s*ine equals *o*pposite over *h*ypotenuse, *c*os equals *a*djacent over *h*ypotenuse, and *t*an equals *o*pposite over *a*djacent. The following couplet gives the first twelve digits of *pi*:

Sir, I send a rhyme excelling
In perfect truth and rigid spelling.

The number of letters in each word is the required digit: 3.14159275358.

The most powerful *aide-memoire* of all, though, is a story. You can weave the list of items to be remembered into a fantastic tale of the Dungeons-and-Dragons type, or you can simply associate each item on the list to be remembered with an element of a story. This actually works. It seems that stories almost remember themselves, coming back to us with such facility that they can easily bring along with them a few extra items of information as well. So potent is story that in preliterate societies, in childhood and in religion most of the really important information is preserved and transmitted in story form. Stories simply stick in the mind better than anything else.

Stories stick so well that we are tempted to think that they are somehow natural, that there are real stories out there apart from us. This, however, is not the case. Stories depend on language, and language is human. We make up all the stories, for our own purposes. We narrate the world, that is, we produce the world, made intelligible within our stories about it. Apart from our interpretative activity, our needs, our language and our story-telling there is only what Aristotle calls 'prime matter', white noise. There is no form out there until language comes along and imposes it. Because we use language and live in time, we *must* tell stories. Elapsing but empty and unstructured time is a nightmare, something horrifying and unthinkable. The mercy of language is not just that it has meaning, but also that it takes time (and makes time, too). People say that in an otherwise empty room even the flickering of a living fire and the ticking of a clock are companionable. They pass the time. Language has the highest degree of that quality. It forms and makes bearable temporality itself. It defers the Void. Stories keep at bay the darkness of a long winter evening.

It is very apt that in the primal story, the story of creation, language sounds in the Void on the very first day. God says 'Let there be light'. He divides the light from the darkness, and calls the light Day and the darkness Night. So the evening and the morning are the first day. People sometimes comment that it seems to them incongruous that day and night should have been created before the creation of the Sun and the Earth. Before the Sun and the Earth existed, they object, the words 'day' and 'night' could have had no meaning. But I am suggesting that this is not a very bright observation. What we should rather notice is that the story pictures language as ringing out amidst the primal chaos, and that the very first line of division it draws is the one that starts to structure time. At least now there's a linear on-off rhythm: day, night, day, night. We are getting somewhere. The story continues with spatial divisions, the separations of Heaven from Earth on day two, and of Land from Sea on day three. The cyclical time of the calendar is fixed on day four, in preparation for animals on day five and humankind on day six. So on the first four days the story is concerned to establish the framework: linear time, the vertical axis (Heaven-Earth), the horizontal axis (land-sea), and cyclical time (the heavenly bodies). And we have to have narrative, because narrative alone can do more than merely register the tick-tock passage of time. Narrative fills time with meaning and structures it. Narrative produces filled time. Of course narrative can only temporarily (lit.) defer loss, for eventually the darkness must close in again. But for now, that postponement is a mercy. It is life itself; it is the breathing space within which we live.

So story structures time and the world, and keeps darkness and death at bay – at least for a while. We are listening to Scheherazade again, putting off death by telling tales through the night. Narrative, only narrative, conquers darkness and the Void.

Since the Enlightenment our cosmological stories have changed a little. We now tell new and very complex stories about the Big

Bang, cosmic evolution, the history of the earth and biological evolution. But it is still we who do all the storytelling, and there is still nothing logically prior to stories. Language still forms time and stories fill it, as before. Science has not greatly changed the situation. The world remains fictional, as it must. All that has happened is that one story has receded somewhat in prominence, and others have come forward to take its place. Evidently the new stories are nowadays found to work better, at least for certain specialized purposes. But it was we alone who told both the old stories and the new. Outside our stories there is still nothing but formlessness. So the classical binary opposition between truth and fiction was a mistake. I can't say it was an *error*, and indeed I am not even sure that I can say it was a *mistake*, for such terms can only confirm the priority of truth. The very use of the word 'truth' seems to imply that there is something true out there that true statements are true of or true to, and in a similar way the very use of the word 'fiction' seems to imply a true, non-fictional background by contrast with which our fictions are merely fictitious. But we should not be wishing to postulate any such background, not really even of prime matter or white noise, nor even of nothingness. These are all un-things. So long as we still feel the need to mention them, or use language in such ways as to seem to be conjuring them up, we remain stuck in old thinking. We ought to have got free of all that. We ought to be thinking in the new way, which is thinking truly outsidelessly.

So we may begin by suggesting that if indeed stories come first in making the world intelligible and memorable, then the old binary contrast between the true and the fictional must be a mistake. Fiction goes all the way down. Fiction comes first. First the world has got to be fictioned into existence from nothing by some kind of story – religious, cosmological, evolutionary, historical or whatever – and only then can we find a place for talk of truth and falsity, relative to the world as thus produced within the story. Fiction logically precedes factuality, and then after fiction, and relative to the world it has established, come along theories, evidences, arguments, points of view, alliances and oppositions. Everything is now in place. We have a working

world. What else do we need; what else could there be? So first
we suggest that the old binary contrast between the really true
and the merely fictitious was a mistake – and then we try to
exorcize the spooks that both expressions presuppose and
imply. We have to get rid of the bogey of a realistic ontology, the
notion that there is something out there prior to and independent of our language and our stories, and against which they can
be checked. As long as we think in that old way, our thinking
has not yet become truly free, clear, playful and outsideless.
We've got to return science into its own theories, religion into its
own stories and rituals – and history into its own varied
narratives.

(b) Moral fables

A person's life-story is a moral fable. As we have seen, some
genres are quite openly essays in self-justification: they include
the speech for the defence, the apologia and the political
memoir. In other cases, people want to make a kind of sermon
out of what life has taught them. The man in the bar who is so
keen to tell you his history wants very much to get across to
others the bit of practical wisdom that his life has taught him.
Everyone seems to have some such lesson for humanity, a lesson
in which the teller's very identity is bound up with the message
he burns to impart and the tale he has to tell. By way of
explaining this strange equation of selfhood, narrative and
moral, I have suggested that stories are highly angled and
perspectival. They invite us to identify ourselves with a leading
character, aligning ourselves with and sharing, as we read, his
responses, actforms and values. The stock phrase for this – and
it's a good one – is, 'Look at it my way'. Precisely. Stories are
highly persuasive, and if I have really listened to that man in the
bar then I really have looked at it his way. I have indeed felt just
as he does; it is as for a while if he and I have been one person.
    Historical narratives too are socially instructive moral fables.
In a slightly backhanded or sidelong way, they reflect and
comment on our current anxieties. At this point realists will
inevitably chip in with the observation that historians are

'constrained by evidence'. By this they mean that doings, proper names and place names that figure in historical narratives have to be crosslinked with occurrences of those same names and so forth in generally-recognized documentary sources. The train of events in the historian's story needs to be in the generally-accepted chronological sequence. Furthermore, the story told must explain the events in a way that conforms to publicly-acknowledged canons of plausibility. The reader expects a narrative which harmonizes with her general expectations about the way the world works and the motives for human action. But all this I readily allow: no writer on the philosophy of history can reasonably deny that historians are indeed constrained by evidence in the three respects just specified.

However, this does not do enough to establish historical realism, or the objectivity of historical knowledge. Every politician of whatever party commenting on current events, every advocate making out a case before a court, every leader-writer and commentator – in short, everyone who makes out a case in public and hopes to be taken seriously – must conform to what are in effect those same three criteria. Of course, you must appeal to the record, you must accept the generally-recognized chronology of events, and you must not make wildly implausible explanatory claims. If you do not wish to be thought fringe or be dismissed as barking mad, then indeed you must endeavour to appear reasonable. But this is not sufficient to establish realism. For the experience of lawcourts, parliaments, the publishing business and so on shows that an immense variety of opinions, including many contradictories, can all be made to appear reasonable by a competent advocate. If being 'constrained by evidence' means only borrowing bits of material from the public record, in the right chronological order and joined up by plausible causal links (and I suggest that that is exactly what it *does* mean), then I fear that life in a modern pluralistic democracy shows that it's not sufficient to establish a common ground of agreed objective public knowledge.

Why is this? It is because 'evidence' is always already selected and angled. Evidence isn't evidence at all until some thesis has been put forward for it to support or refute, as the case may be.

Evidence has got to be evidence for or against something. And as daily experience shows, the same bit of material can very often be subpoenaed into giving evidence both for p and for not-p. Notoriously, theories elicit their own evidence and bully it into pointing their way. When I see that my opponent has nobbled some cherished bit of evidence that I had been hoping to use for my purposes, and is brazenly using it for her own, I am apt to accuse her of 'selective quotation'. But what other sort of quotation is there?

Furthermore, these considerations apply also to whatever is currently thought of as being the public record (or 'the primary sources'). The so-called 'original' material is itself also an angled selection, and so on all the way back. The sources are already 'intertextual', made out of the interplay of many earlier stories. Pure and uncontaminated factuality is never reached and cannot be reached, because the very first eyewitness already had an angle. Interpretation goes all the way back.

Now historians are by definition interested parties. They need to have axes to grind. If an historian has got a good idea for a book, that must mean that she's got some interesting moral or political thesis to propound, and is going to illustrate it from historical sources. So her quotation is going to be selective and tendentious. It can scarcely be otherwise.

Decency, however, requires that the historian must not appear to be too manipulative. An historical narrative must not be grossly tendentious. It has to be both believable and at the same time artistically satisfying. All the data and details adduced have to be plausibly explained, and they must all be relevant. As in a good novel or detective story, all the detail that is introduced must contribute to the organic unity of the whole work. Although the book as a whole needs to have a strong thesis, readers hate to feel that they are being bludgeoned. What's more, it is artistically crude. In a well-made history-book the reader is therefore allowed space in which, as they say, to draw his own conclusions. Under Stalin, any Russian play or film about a great autocrat from the past such as Boris Godounov or Ivan the Terrible had an obvious contemporary resonance for its audience. The point did not need to be laboured. So the historian can well afford to handle the bearing of the past upon the present in a veiled and delicate manner.

However, these special artistic constraints upon the historian don't have the effect of making her any the less selective and tendentious. Quite the contrary: they require her to add extra literary qualities of artistic craftsmanship and low cunning.

The upshot of this is that we have quite clearly abandoned the early-nineteenth-century ideal of encyclopaedic positive history. Instead we recognize that historical works are inevitably and quite rightly tendentious. They are artistically constructed as moral fables, checkable against acknowledged documentary sources indeed, but recognizing that no sources are absolutely 'primary', and in any case quite rightly utilizing them in a highly selective way. For the merit of a work of history depends entirely on the artistic skill with which the materials used are selected, angled and ordered in support of a thesis. Narratives are 'kinds of theories', says A.C. Danto;[1] the story leads to a conclusion which may be a piece of practical or moral wisdom, or perhaps a generalization in politics or economics. It is the book's *raison d'etre*, for the work is unlikely to be written and will certainly not sell unless its thesis is of interest to the writer and her contemporaries.

Once again, *we* tell all the stories, *we* narrate the world, and the stories we tell both reflect and further our interests. There is no story out there; our narrative constructions of reality are produced by way of setting up a moral framework for us to inhabit, and scripting parts for ourselves either to play or to play at playing.

The perspectival character of history-writing seems now to be widely accepted. Consider some such large and general social issue as the origins and significance of modern nationalism, the means by which governments seek to secure and maintain the consent of the governed, the relations between women and men, the decline of religion, the difference between society's dominant creed and the beliefs actually prevailing among the common people, and the history of childhood. The past is dense, and these topics are all of them many-faceted and disputable. We are relativists insofar as we now recognize that on any one of these topics many good books can be written and are being written to prove radically divergent theses. There is no single truth any more, and our understanding of an issue actually needs to be enhanced by careful consideration of conflicting angles upon it and seemingly contradictory theses about it – without any right answer or final truth ever being reached. All we have and all we will ever have is a conflict of perspectives or viewpoints, but the *level* of the debate may be higher or lower, and that is what counts. Indeed, one might usefully define the historian's purpose in writing as an attempt to raise the level of public debate about a contemporary issue, by telling a parable set in the past about it.

(c) Master narratives

In *Mimesis*, Erich Auerbach draws a striking contrast between two books, the *Odyssey* and the Hebrew Bible.[2] The *Odyssey*, he says, is a book to enjoy for the way it allows one to enter an enchanted world. True, it does not neglect to celebrate certain vital qualities of character that the Greeks saw themselves as possessing, like endurance, seamanship and cunning. But it is not a morally-aggressive work that harasses its reader. It is an escape, a book that lets you forget your cares. In complete contrast, the Old Testament is an imperious work that drags the reader into its world and seeks to constrain him to situate his own life within its master-narrative. It is authoritative and revelatory: you the reader experience it as making you part of its plot. Scripture scripts you. Where the *Odyssey* is recreation, scripture is re-creation.

Thus Auerbach, providing a good late example of just how seductive the idea of a master-narrative can be. He dreams of a book free from the limitations of merely human books, a book that is not just a book but is *the* Book.[3] This absolute Book must tell a story that is not merely one more human fiction but the real World-Story itself, written by the world's Author. The Book will be world-shaped, just as the world in its whole course from Creation to Judgment is book-shaped. Text and Cosmos both have a beginning, a crux in the middle, and an end. The utterance of one and the same eternal God both made the world and is written down in the Book, so that world and Book are the same message fixed in two different media. Live punctiliously by the Book, and you live the life pre-scribed for you. You get life right. Everything becomes rooted in the Centre of all things: your life-story, the narrative in the Book, the world-story, and God's eternal Will are lined up and locked together in concentric circles. When everything is in accord like that, everything is concentred, and you live in the Truth.

Auerbach was trying to say that the Bible is a book different in kind from all other books, and I have spelled out in a little more detail just what is being claimed here. The master-narrative is not just a mythical or archetypal pattern, to be re-enacted any number of times: it is a drama whose one and only script is scripture and whose one and only performance is human history – of which your life now is a part. No doubt in other societies one can find national myths, communal and institutional narratives known to everyone which give people a shared world-view, shared values and patterns of behaviour, and a shared sense of their historical origins and destiny. No doubt, too, there have been many faiths and ideologies which have seemed to those under their sway to hold the key to the future of humanity. But the Holy scriptures still provide the strongest of all forms of the idea of a master-narrative. Not a story we made up but the story that makes us up, conscripting us into its plot; writing God into every step of our lives and every step of our lives into the plan of God.

If you have a master-narrative to live by you feel guided; you feel upborne. You know that your name is written in the Book of Life. There is something a little like *déjà-vu* in the knowledge that every step you take has been foreseen and predestined. Even liberals and marxists, whose master-narratives were relatively weak, could feel they were surf-riding the rolling waves that they called Progress and History; but the early Calvinist experience was far stronger. The great Story of God's plan of salvation had become ontologized. It was no longer only a text: it was reality itself. It was still recapitulated for you in scripture every day and in the weekly sermon, but in your daily life you were actually living it. You had a part in it already written for you.

Yet there is an acute paradox lurking here. In order to set up the idea of a master-narrative in the first place, I needed a very clear-cut line between language and reality, words and things; but as we explored how the idea of a master-narrative works itself out in practice, the line was transgressed and eventually disappeared altogether. We began with the ultra-realism typical of most religious orthodoxy, but we seemed to end in idealism or even expressivism. Language, in the form of the biblical text, was taking over reality completely.

For consider: in order to say that this Book (Bible, Qu'ran or whatever) is not a mere humanly invented thing but is the very book of books, we must say that it was written by God, that it has been revealed to us by God, and that it is a perfect fulfilment of God's plan to make known to us his creative and saving purpose. What is in the Book is not just any old story, but the one and only objective and story-transcending Truth about God's eternal decree and about our origins, our religious history and our destiny. So to set up the Book's authority in the first place I need a strongly realistic theology, both of the God (independent of the Book) who is the Book's Author, and of the cosmic drama of redemption (also independent of the Book) to which the Book bears true witness. The Book has got to be, in the strongest sense, true *to* the mind of its Author and true *of* the cosmic drama that he has set up. For the book thus to get God and his world exactly right, language has got to be completely masterable and God has got to be its master, so that in this text he really has put down precisely what he intended to say to us. And language has also got to be capable of representing events exactly or perfectly, so that the Book can be for us humans a true report and an infallible guide to life. If the Book is to be one hundred per cent reliable, then it must describe the past and future saving acts of God in history *exactly*. Language must then be both completely masterable and capable of being completely adequate.

From this it follows that people who are committed to a very strong belief in the scriptural revelation of truth are thereby committed also to ultra-realism. Reformed Protestants, Muslims, Orthodox Jews and others need ultra-realism in order to explain how a chain of sentences can both be fully adequate as an expression of God's mind, and also fully adequate as a theological account of how things have gone, are going and will go with humankind in the real world. By 'full adequacy' we mean thoroughgoing literalism, which is the doctrine that sentences can both have exactly the same form and content as the prelinguistic mental intentions they express, and also can exactly copy the objective course of salvific events out in the translinguistic real world of human history. Literal truth is a point-by-point exact match, both of words to thoughts and of words to things.

It is at just this point that realism goes over the top, and suddenly collapses. The general principle at work here is very simple. For many purposes we make copies, maps and replicas. We try to improve them, and this gives rise to the belief in the possibility of a perfect copy. Unfortunately, when a copy becomes *perfect* we can no longer make the distinction between the original and the copy. They become indistinguishable – and the very notion of copying breaks down. Thus copies, maps and replicas actually need to remain secondary and imperfect, for we run into a paradox if we try to imagine a really perfect one.

In the case of the ultra-realist view of revelation, the paradox arises as follows. Language is always secondary, metaphorical and fictive. It defers death and nothingness by telling tales, but it only defers them. It never quite delivers 'presence', or the real absolutely. It cannot. But people who want a master-narrative want there to be language that is, impossibly, free from the inescapable limitations of all language, they want there to be a book that is more than just another book, and they want there to be a story that is not just a story but is *the* Story, a story that is so much more than a story that it prescribes and replicates the exact shape of Reality itself. Yet even to state this idea of a Master Story so potent that it is not a mere story but coincides with the movement of real life itself, a story that has my own actual life already written into it – even to state this idea, I must *both* sharply distinguish writing from real life *and* obliterate that same distinction. I've got to say, 'Here's a text, a story written in a book, which supernaturally and miraculously gets our life absolutely *right*. Yes, the book has the literary form of a many-faceted epic theological drama, but it gets the story so right that the denotation of words like story, drama and plan moves out of the text and into the life-world, and God becomes the Author of the World as well as of the Book. Actual cosmic history from beginning to end thus becomes *itself* the scripted epic theological drama that the Book describes.' But now the distinction between language and reality has become effaced, because we are starting to see the supposed real world and human life as mere literary projections. The real has now become itself literary, itself a drama scripted in advance, and therefore barely distinguishable from the Book that contains its script. We were so determined to have a super-powerful book of words that guaranteed reality that we ended up with a reality that was made just of and by words.

Now look in the opposite direction, and consider the claim that language is completely masterable, and God is so completely its master that he makes the written text a perennially perfect expression of his mind towards us. But if God's self-expression is indeed thus complete and final, then nothing of God can remain unexpressed – and he vanishes into his text. It is all that there is of him, for we have no way of saying that he is anything more than this. He has said it all.

Once again, in order to explain the claim, 'This Book is a revelation of God's mind', we must make an initial distinction between certain mental or spiritual things – thoughts, dispositions, intentions, volitions – and their secondary expression in words. We portray words as clothing, conveying, expressing or embodying thoughts. Then we claim that one particular chain of sentences expresses thoughts so perfectly that they come through without any distortion or contamination. But in saying this we have again effaced the distinction between thoughts and their verbal expression. The text is the mind and the mind is the text. Divinity himself has become 'divinity' in the sense of 'sacred letters'.

Thus the real disappears twice over. God vanishes into the

text of scripture, and the text of scripture is now seen as producing the 'real world' of the believer's experience. In this way ultra-realism abruptly turns into textualism, the world as nothing but writing. And in retrospect we can now see the entire history of scriptural religion, Jewish, Christian and Islamic, as in perpetual but concealed oscillation between realism and textualism.

No, it is stranger even than that: it is rather that the very peak of realism in a writer like Calvin is precisely the point at which we see textualism breaking through. Calvin is a humanist, a man of letters, a rhetorician and lawyer. Just when his vocabulary is at its most objectivist, being most heteronomous and most concerned to make us the playthings of absolute Power, it is also at its most literary.[4] The language of decree, statute, command-ment, law, ordinance, predestination, plan, revelation and so on functions to suggest that God has fixed reality in writing. If indeed reality itself is a drama or story that God has scripted beforehand, then the real is a creation of language – as in the law, which is the paradigm case of a subject where language creates reality. It is noticeable that devout people themselves say that when you live by the Book your life becomes a meaningful story; that is, you have turned your own life into a kind of fiction. To desire religious meaningfulness in life is nothing but to demand the dramatization of life, the assurance that our life has been scripted in advance. So the distinction between language and reality, the literary plan of Salvation and its historical enactment, gets effaced. When the very being of the world is held within scriptural text and religious doctrine, realism has become idealism because, as they say, 'scripture must be fulfilled'. The action must follow the script. Even in common speech there are many idioms that stress the superior and prior reality of text: for example, the wise American advice, 'God is love, but get it in writing'. We have. Scripture is the script for lives in which God is love.

Along these lines, then, we can readily show the close affinity between scriptural religion and 'textualism', the recent philosophy of writing. For whether they like it or not, those who claim to have a primary and exclusive revelation of saving truth in a

Book that gives them the Story they live by cannot be very far removed from those who say that there is nothing outside the text. The most extreme theological realists, that is, the scriptural fundamentalists, and the most extreme theological anti-realists are both of them products of the modern period, and a lot closer to each other than is usually recognized. They differ, obviously, in their understanding of language. But how in the present dispute does this difference emerge and lead them to part company?

Clearly, the conservative believer experiences his master-narrative as producing his world, surrounding him and constraining him. He experiences, he reads his life as scripture writ large. Could he concede that this is just a textually generated effect? Can he be content to say simply that his Bible has made his world for him? Not quite, because as we have remarked all traditional believers in master-narratives are strong realists. It is not just a matter of the biblical words being self-fulfilling: there is also a real God out there, actively fulfilling his word. That is, realists always have some form of belief in Grace, in the sense that they maintain that there are forces for good at work out there independent of us, and perhaps also in the sense that they think the constitution of things out there and prior to us tends to make sense and to be friendly to the good. Marxists think (or thought) that laws of historical development are operative and tending towards the victory of socialism independently of our efforts. Liberals think that the world is knowable, that knowledge can be built up and systematized, and that the growth of knowledge is compatible with and even favours an increase in overall human goodness and well-being. Most religious believers of whatever faith believe in the possibility for the individual of a good and holy life and final salvation, and also in an ultimate and cosmic triumph of goodness.

Old-style believers were therefore all of them metaphysical optimists. They find an analogy between scripture and the life-world because (as they say) the same God made both, and not merely because scripture forms the way they construct their picture of the life-world. Consider now the position of a modern non-realist believer. She may choose the same master-narrative, allowing it to produce her world and living a life guided by it. But she does not suppose that there is anything out there in the world, apart from and prior to the text of the master-narrative, that is in the least friendly to her faith and lifework. Obviously not, for she is a textualist. There is only the great Story and the life-world that it produces. There is nothing out there except (if you wish) that formless unthing, 'white noise'. Thus the non-realist believer does not believe in what I called 'Grace', in the sense of something out there in the constitution or the workings of the world that is antecedently and independently friendly. No, there's nothing like that. A modern non-realist Marxist has to strive for the victory of socialism, not because the victory of socialism is in any way inevitable (it obviously isn't) but because she thinks it would be a good thing. She wants to live by this story, but unlike traditional realistic believers she doesn't think that the objective nature of things does anything to privilege this story. It is only a story she lives by, and she knows there are no stories out there. We wrote all the stories, and we produce all the interpretations and enactments of them. So for the non-realist, if you want it to be true then you yourself have got to make it come true.

In an influential essay that appeared in 1979, J.-F. Lyotard described 'the postmodern condition' as the state of people for whom all the master-narratives have broken down.[5] I suggest we should read this as meaning that the old kind of realistic, dogmatic and exclusive belief in the cosmically privileged status of just one master-narrative – one's own, of course – has broken down. It has broken down because we now see that there is nothing out there, independent of all the master-narratives, that does anything to privilege any one of them. They are all just optional fictions to live by. All views of the world and ways of life are games. You are free to play which you like, or none. There is no constraining truth.

Lyotard went on to say that the breakdown of all the master-narratives was a crisis, because in the past all human strivings had in the end been justified ultimately by reference to master-narratives. Scholarship and scientific research, for example, had been justified by reference to the Enlightenment master-narrative which claimed that the progressive increase and systematization of knowledge would enlighten and liberate humanity at large. Political activity was justified in terms of its contribution to the future triumph of socialism. Religious activity saved souls and helped build up the Kingdom of God – and so on. Actions were justified in terms of their contribution to goals defined in master-narratives. The breakdown of master-narratives produces a crisis of legitimation, in the sense that a whole range of institutions and activities seem suddenly to lose their point. If my present efforts are neither going to contribute to any greater end nor to be conserved or recorded, why bother? Nothing has any long-term point any more.

Are things as bad as Lyotard seems to suggest? No, because the point of a game is internal to the playing of the game. The thought that games are extrinsically pointless does not in the least diminish the dedication with which people play them. More generally, the losses we have suffered may not be so grievous as some people suggest. There is nothing out there which privileges just one master-narrative, not even my own favoured candidate, so I know that I must give up making exclusive and dogmatic Truth-claims. We now need the old notion of objective Truth only in order to state that because there is none, we are pensioning it off. Instead, pluralism, tolerance and play: but is that such a bad thing? No aggressive proselytizing. Instead, the same sort of easy-going free-for-all in ideologies and faiths that we already have in the arts and literature. Why not? Contrary to what Lyotard suggests, you can still live by your preferred master-narrative if you choose, and you can make of it what you choose. You have indeed lost your traditional sense of a right and a duty to seek to impose your beliefs upon others, but then nowadays we all of us seem to be giving that up. The knowledge that in the long run the Void must win can be turned to our spiritual advantage if we use it to make our view of life lighter and more playful, more Zen. Admittedly we have given up the old realistic belief in Grace, in the sense of something out there working to vindicate you and your beliefs. But we can still have the experience of Grace, providing that we don't mind acknowledging that it is textually generated. You can make your own fiction come true, and feel its truth coming back at you. It can be *as if* there were Grace, rather as during the playing of a game small benefits (or penalties) may be received in accordance with the rules. Such benefits can be real enough within the game and relative to its objects, but they cannot be cashed outside the context of the game.

It must be confessed that when we understand that our own religious experiences are not given to us from outside, but are merely produced from within us by the story we have chosen to live by, there is a certain loss of the old innocence and vividness. But if innocence and vividness of experience were what is most to be desired, then we would all wish to be schizophrenics and epileptics, for they have the most wonderfully intense and vivid experiences of anyone. So perhaps we should not regret the fact that as we become saner and nore sceptical what people call 'experiences' largely disappear. There are compensating gains.

A point about historicality needs to be made in conclusion. We described as realism or as 'Grace' the belief that something out there is at work helping things along independently of our efforts, and thoughtfully doing so in such a way as to tend to vindicate our master-narrative. A simple example is the way many Marxists have thought that the failure of capitalism and the triumph of socialism were inevitable anyway, quite apart from our own efforts to bring them about. The very nature of things, it seemed, was eager both to help us along and to confirm our beliefs.

That particular naivety is what we have recently lost. With it we have also lost the apologetic mileage we used to think there was in the appeal to history. Can we really take a journey back into the past, track down some upstanding and unadorned chaps called 'objective historical facts', and persuade them to time-travel with us back to the present day so that they can offer public testimony to the truth of our master-narrative? No, we can not. We cannot do it in relation to any historical theory, not even the least contentious; so we certainly cannot do it in this case. When we stop to think about it, we see that it was naive of us to have supposed that a witness from the past could speak today in a voice both fully independent and exclusively committed to our own cause. We should not ask for such a dream witness. We must do without the belief that something quite independent of our favoured master-narrative, something which we call objective historical fact, can be called upon to validate it. Future belief will have to be cheerfully fictionalist. And so, of course, will the argument of the present book.

(d) The perfect life

So future belief will have to be cheerfully fictionalist, will it? We cannot appeal to history for justification, nor can we believe in capital-T Truth? What then are the implications for the belief that there has been lived a perfect life to show us how we should live?

Consider the following story. His father was a shadowy figure, but his mother was important to him. Even before he was born, dreams and portents warned her that she was a chosen vessel through whom someone unique would enter the world. Further portents attended his birth, and there were some hints during his childhood of his future destiny. But it was in the prime of his young manhood that he declared his vocation. He renounced the family ties, the status and even the clothing that had so far been his, and took up the life of a poor wandering teacher.

The forces of evil felt an impending threat to their power, and tested him during his wilderness period. But they could not shake him. He gathered a small band of disciples who went about with him. He was so pure that women could not threaten him, and he was kind to them when they approached him, as they often did. The time came for there to be a revelation of the spiritual perfection he had attained, and it took place on a sacred mountain, or beneath a sacred tree. There followed the years of fulfilment, the closing period of his work, during which he advised his followers and prepared them for his departure from the world. Finally his hour arrived and he passed away, rising through the heavens to the cosmic bliss in which his followers still see him as living.

It is the standard biography of a 'theios aner', a divine man, the founder of an Eastern religion. The Buddha, Mahavira and many others conform to this pattern very closely.[6] So do Jesus and other figures of Mediterranean antiquity, though in the case of Jesus other themes are spliced in as well – the martyred Jewish prophet, and the dying and rising Lord of life.

Not all religious founders are of the wandering holy man type. Some are very different: for example, the wise woman and prophetess figure such as Mary Baker Eddy, Miki[7] and Alice Lenshina. A very important type in antiquity was the national leader, lawgiver, warrior, prophet and recipient of revelation, a type of figure best exemplified by Moses and Muhammad. The national leader is always married, whereas the holy man is always seen as celibate.

In order to stress his purity and spiritual perfection the holy man's biography makes him as different as possible from us. He is not contaminated by earthly ties of any kind. He is seen as having been sexless, homeless and jobless: chaste, itinerant and mendicant. He cannot really mix, nor be the product of mixture. For this reason he cannot quite be seen as the product of normal human sexual intercourse, for that involves the commingling of male and female flesh. So his father is pushed into the background, and his mother becomes just a pure vessel to carry him. She is impregnated through her ear, side or thigh. The child descends into her from the supernatural world already perfectly formed, so that he needs only to be nurtured and grow larger inside her. After that the manner in which she gives him birth is also supernaturally protected from incurring any kind of impurity; and now he is safely launched into the world, a wonderchild quite unlike any ordinary human being.

So it goes on: evidently we are in a magical narrative world in which anything can happen, a world in which symbolic and imaginative requirements shape the course of events and dictate what the truth must have been.

In the origins of Christianity the process of religious fictionalization, or doctrinal development as theologians prefer to call it, is particularly well documented. We have four canonical Gospels and large numbers of apocryphal ones, so that we can see the imaginative transformation of Jesus at various stages, and going in various directions. In Mark's Gospel Jesus is still a human figure. He is the Messiah-designate, with a very exalted mission. He is already caught up in the ferocious stress of an apocalyptic conflict with the powers of evil. He is dark, tragic, driven and destined, but he is nonetheless entirely human, human enough to be often stormy, vehement and quick-tempered. The narrative shows no particular wish to purify him either by making him calm and tranquil, or by denying his natural human begetting and birth.

By contrast, in Luke Jesus is much calmer. He is more loving, prays much more often, and moves more smoothly along his predestined path to glory. The element of pleasing folk-supernaturalism is also more prominent, and Mary conceives him virginally. The apocryphal gospels and subsequent mediaeval doctrine and iconography develop steadily further in the same direction.

Finally, in the Gospels of John and Thomas most of Jesus' utterance is that of a heavenly visitor to this world. His status is so exalted that popular supernaturalism has become inappropriate, and the narrative does not really wish to involve itself in any speculation about his fleshly origins. He does not have a human beginning, and he is not a human product. He is simpl and wholly of God.

In all this there is an obvious irony to be pointed out. In its barest pre-narrative facticity, human life is meaningless: indeed, it is not yet human at all. Meaning depends upon narrative. So to give human life meaning, we must start telling stories about it. We've got to narrate it, that is, to fictionalize it. We alone make meaning, and religious significance in particular is fictional, that is, produced within narrative. Jesus has to be mythicized, assimilated to some standard religious story-form, in order to become an object of faith. And this we see happening in the Gospels. How ironical it is then that many people are so insistent upon the 'literal historicity' of the Virgin Birth and the Resurrection of Jesus! They muddy the waters twice over, first because naked, outside-language objectivity is an empty, meaningless unthing that nobody should want to get back to;

and secondly because religious miracles, doctrines and meanings get all their weight and their point from their narrative settings in the fictional realm where they live. The search for a pre-fictional truth or objectivity is a mistake. Nothing has meaning and *a fortiori* nothing is real or religious, until it is fictionalized.

A consequence of all this is that when we scan the life of a saint or holy person, looking for a pattern of meaning that we might be able to pick up and make our own, we cannot expect to find anything but what we ourselves have previously put there. That is how it is, and there is no cause for complaint about it.

A parable: I once briefly visited Arctic mountains so remote and inhospitable that they have never been inhabited, nor even explored. These mountains were above the treeline, barren, unmapped and unnamed. They seemed to me horrible and I had no wish to climb them. With no human language spread over them, they were repellent and meaningless. A popular *façon de parler* suggests that just having names would have been enough to cheer them up. The idea is that proper names give language reference, and are enough both to hook language on to the world and to tame the world enough to make it describable. This, however, is not so. Reference presupposes stories. Names familiarize the world only by being used in stories within which they signify locations and roles. For sounds to stick to those mountains as used and usable *names*, they would have to figure in stories about groups of people exploring, mapping and generally spreading over the area. Best of all is to walk in a place like the Lake District, where you are walking in literature. There is meaning all about you.

So it is that by telling stories upon stories we build up our world, ourselves and our history as language and in language. As animals mark out their territories with urine and other scents, so we cover over the world with language; and as dogs live in a world of smells so we live in a world of words. By symbolically 'marking' and structuring experience, and above all by telling stories, we have slowly turned a barren wilderness of white noise into a habitable world.

In a veiled way, many religious myths are about this process by which barren chaos is made into a friendly habitable cosmos. They are our most powerful and general communal stories. They produce the main outlines of our human selfhood, community, values and cosmology.

So the problem here is the same as the one we met in discussing realism. How are we to explain the obstinate and seemingly incoherent insistence of the orthodox upon objectivity, whether described as metaphysical, historical or literal? Why is objective reality, or whatever it is they think they are after, supposed to be a Good Thing?

I need an error theory, for the following reason. I take the democratic view of truth, meaning and value. Nothing absolute or purely objective determines any truth, or the meaning of any word, or any value. All these things depend only upon an historically-evolved and changeable human consensus. If we have no access to anything extra-historical nor to any absolute vocabulary, then we are bound to put our trust in the way most people, most of the time, use words. That in general is my policy. There is no alternative to it: here am I, writing English. But if so, I have real difficulty in suggesting that many or most people are badly wrong for much of the time, and in a matter of great consequence. I will need a theory to explain how the error I am postulating is produced and maintained.

In the case of moral realism, the answer is fairly easy to see. Since the Second World War morality has become thoroughly historicized. Social history and the history of ideas have made everyone aware of the way moral values change over time. We have seen how the morality of attitudes to people of other races and creeds, of the treatment of our physical and biological environment, and of the politics of sex has changed radically during the past four decades. Almost everyone knows now that moral values are produced by and embodied in our historically-developing human conversation. Yet we continue to use a number of objectivist idioms, as when we say that such-and-such is utterly or absolutely wrong or evil. Why? An error theory to explain this must say that we use such language partly because it has come down to us from the past, partly as a way of expressing the strength of our moral convictions and our sense of their over-riding importance, and partly by way of trying to pass our values on to the young. We are in a novel and difficult situation, trying to reconcile our traditional and entirely justified sense of the overwhelming importance to us of our moral values with our strange new awareness of their contingency, instability, and even perhaps ephemerality. During this interim period a certain amount of inconsistency is understandable. Such, briefly, is our error theory with respect to the continuing use of the vocabulary of moral realism.[8]

What then will be our error theory to account for the belief, admittedly widespread both among religious conservatives and fundamentalists, and amongst the great mass of nostalgic fellow-travellers, that religious truth is something objective, revealed, unchangeable, eternal and divine? Many of the same considerations apply: during the past two centuries critical theology, the history of religions, and, through travel and population movements, greater awareness of other races, have together made us aware of the extent to which religious belief is a human, cultural and changing thing. Yet it is evidently still more difficult for religiously committed people to admit the humanity of religion than it is for morally-serious people to admit the humanity of morality. Apart from traditionalism and institutional drag, the most important factor is the extent to which religious ideologies defend themselves by incorporating built-in blocks to consciousness. Chief of these is an unvoiced but intense belief that some natural language – Latin, Greek, Arabic or Hebrew, perhaps – can be used, *has* been used, with superhuman precision and control, so that it is not in any way eroded, shifted or made obscure by historical change. The text that defines the Truth can be complete and final, with no instability and no contrary undercurrents. On this theory, 'linguistic supernaturalism', depend the ideas of metaphysical realism, a superhuman realm, God as personal, a natural order, scriptural revelation, the immutability of dogma and much, much more. In short, my error theory is that religion so far has depended upon a common mistake about language, a mistake too big for most people to give up. Their desperate attempt in highly unfavourable conditions to maintain this old mistake,

at least in the religious realm, is what the world calls
fundamentalism. They are struggling to fix and control language
so that it can continue to be God's speech, resist historical
change, compass absolutes and express pure Truth. Revealed
religion requires language to be a superhuman and heavenly
thing.

A corollary of all this is that received religious formulations
are treated as sacrosanct. It cannot be admitted that their
vocabulary is historically conditioned. We are committed in
perpetuity to the particular way that Jesus happened to get
fictionalized by the early Christians. Yet if this were indeed the
case it would be a disaster, as should have been obvious in the
opening paragraphs of this section. The Gospels, and perhaps
especially those of Matthew, Luke and John, surround Jesus
with a mythology that has only quite recently come to seem
morally repulsive and deeply alien. In particular, ancient ideas
of holiness and a holy life required one to avoid sexual, social
and economic *mixing*, and were very profoundly misogynistic. It
is hard to imagine that those ideas could now be reinstated. It is
more plausible to suggest that the old religions must either
change or perish.

At this point feminist theologians such as Daphne Hampson
say that Christianity is stuck with a vocabulary, with doctrines
and with Gospels that are incorrigibly sexist. Women must leave
Christianity, because it cannot be changed as much as it needs to
be changed without ceasing to be itself.[9]

On all the three standard interpretations of Christianity,
conservative, liberal-critical and fundamentalist, Dr Hampson is
right. Established views of what Christianity is don't allow it
enough scope for change for it to be able to survive; and
something similar is true of several other world religions.

A more literary view of what Christianity is, however, gives
some hope. If you treat a religion as a mythology, a large body
of stories, then you can understand how those stories may be
selectively told and retold with very different morals. A familiar
example is the Arthurian cycle. Perhaps originally the stories
were about a family curse; incest, adultery and their inevitable
long-term consequences. But it proved easy to retell such a large

and rich body of tales to convey numerous other messages, about romantic love, about the quest for the Grail, about the tragic difficulty of attempting to ally might with right, and so on. If the literary imagination working on the Arthur legends can so easily bend them into whatever new shapes new times may require, why should not the same be done with the life of Jesus?

It has been done. During the present century dozens of interesting fictional rewrites of the life of Jesus have been produced by novelists. Reflecting the moral changes of recent generations, these works regularly give Jesus a sex life, make him a dissident and so on. Conservative Christians protest predictably, in the name of historical accuracy and fidelity to the text. But I am saying that the original Jesus – i.e., what we find in Matthew, Mark, Luke and John – is already, and inevitably, thoroughly fictionalized. Through and through, he is there written to express archetypal patterns and period values. What is more, the distinction between fact and interpretation, history and myth, is itself an ideological fiction. We will never reach a purely historical, pre-fictionalized Jesus. There is none to be reached, and we should not even wish to reach such a figure. To be understood at all Jesus must from the very first be described in some particular period vocabulary, with its myths and its values. He is always already mythicized – so nothing stops us from re-mythicizing him in our own way. Until we try, we will not know what the ideal of a holy life might mean today, or what Christ might mean to us today. We need to drop the positivist theory of exegesis as reconstructing the original meaning of the text, and instead accept what the history of Bible-interpretation shows – namely, that exegesis always was and unavoidably is a kind of cursive embroidery, a fictional amplification which can *easily* transform the original text.

People often fail to recognize just how creative exegesis is, but consider the example of slavery, which is legislated for in the Old Testament and taken for granted throughout the Bible. To this day every prayer used and every ritual performed appears at first glance to be celebrating subjection, and glorifying the master-slave relationship in biblical imagery. Yet modern believers have no difficulty at all in down-playing the issue, and in presenting the Bible as a charter of liberation and human rights. If the Bible's acceptance of slavery can thus be overcome, why should not its sexism be similarly dealt with?

(e) The talisman

People still say it can't be done. They say that you cannot hope plausibly to refiction or rewrite the Gospels as drastically as would be necessary. Like it or not, the picture of Jesus as sexless, homeless and jobless, as an ancient holy man living in a man's world, praying to a masculine God, choosing only male disciples to continue his work and so forth, is there and is alien to us. The old idea of the holy as something fearsomely Other is still active in the way the Gospels set out to distance Jesus as much as possible from ordinary secular humanity. He is portrayed as a wandering teacher who has no visible means of support and acknowledges no obligations except to God; he is one who has no time at all for the juggling of rival earthly loyalties that occupies so much of other people's lives. But when religious narrative thus associates holiness with the repudiation of all sexual, local and economic ties, it creates a binary opposition between the sacred and the profane. This in turn downgrades ordinary people and secular life, and therefore attracts protests. Ordinary human life is lived in a continuous to and fro of love and war, 'mixing it'. We are always serving two masters, balancing loyalties. Compromise, mingling and conflict are the very stuff of our experience. Jesus' reported dissociation from any mixture or compromise seems to many people pathological rather than holy, the sign of an excessive fastidiousness and fear of contact with others. It also bears hard upon women, for woman even more than man is a being whose very life and identity have always in the past been defined through her relationships with others. The ancient ideal of holiness seems to privilege men, suggesting that they are relatively holier than women merely because they have usually been more independent, self-sufficient and free to drop everything. Women therefore readily interpret ancient religious thought as having been highly sexist, which while we are following the present line of argument it obviously was.

All these considerations seem to suggest that if in Christianity the figure of Jesus is inseparable from the narratives in the Gospels, and if in the narratives the stories and the values they teach are inseparable, then we will simply not be able to rewrite the Gospels radically enough.

Maybe. Certainly I do not deny that the Evangelists set out to portray Jesus as a profoundly disturbing and anomalous figure, and that they succeeded. But everything can be interpreted in many ways, and the oddity of the traditional Christian picture of Jesus may be read quite differently. Perhaps the point being made by the Evangelists is that Jesus was one of those exceptional beings who somehow cannot help becoming a myth. There are people, places and works of art that are like that; they capture the imagination and attract legends. Stories proliferate around them, and people want to identify with them.

This suggests an alternative explanation of the anomalousness of Jesus. In the earlier discussion we understood the Evangelists to be trying to distance Jesus from ordinary married, working, struggling secular humanity, and thereby to create a binary opposition between his single-minded theocentric holiness and our inferior double-minded lives, immersed in worldly cares. The upshot seemed to be that we were made to feel obscurely guilty for not being able to reach an impossible standard. Lutheranism has indeed interpreted Jesus' teaching along these very lines,[10] attracting the retort that such a Jesus is merely a creator of bad conscience. In a democratic age we are all of us apt to feel that the truly exceptional person merely by existing constitutes a reproach to us, and we may therefore resent him.

On the alternative view, however, the Evangelists' purpose in making Jesus so anomalous was not in the least to make us feel inadequate. We should be guided by a clue from the history of religions, which teaches that the point of the anomalous is not that it is purely and impossibly holy, but rather that it is both holy and unclean at once. It unites opposites in itself, bridging the gulf between two contrasting realms. It is transgressive, disturbing and magical.

Among the objects that are anomalous in this sense are virgins, corpses, midnight and snakes. If that is not miscellaneous enough, try nuns, ladders, one-legged men and mistletoe. Or homosexuals, four-leafed clovers, gateways and puberty. The anomalous is seen as partaking of two different natures: it is both man and woman, today and tomorrow, beast and worm, child and adult, inside and outside, living and dead and so on. The anomalous calls into question the various lines of distinction in terms of which we usually order our world. It may attract anger and disgust, but it can also switch on the imagination and set language moving. It may even be magical and blessed: fair-haired visitors to inland China find themselves being touched for good luck. The anomalous attracts myths because we look for stories to resolve the feeling of uncertainty that it creates.

Because the anomalous is a transitional object linking two realms, it may become a doorway between them, or even a guide and protector that helps us through perilous transitions in our own lives. In this way it comes to be viewed as a mascot, lucky charm, amulet or talisman, and may play a surprisingly large part in childhood. For children are people who are passing very rapidly through a number of difficult transitions as they grow up. They very often become fiercely attached to some object that is their constant companion in testing times. It may be seen sitting on the desk in front of a child during a school examination; it helps the child through, and is frequently glanced at for inspiration. It may have the form of an animal-friend, a toy-demon or monster, or a little freak. It is also a confidant, like a guardian spirit, a fetish or an imaginary friend. The child may speak to it and tell it stories.

In some cases the child's talisman may be a special private magic place to which she or he resorts in times of trouble. All children dream of having a cave or a treehouse to be such a place for them.

The child's behaviour towards its talisman may be connected with its earlier attitude first to the breast, and then to the treasured smelly old blanket of late infancy. It may also look forward to later religious behaviour. Like a god, the talisman is a protector, a resort in time of trouble, a companion and confidant, and above all it helps you to make crossings.

D. W. Winnicott described such children's fetishes as transitional objects, adding a further important point: we form attachments to these objects not just because they help us through times of transition in our own lives, but also because they regularly function to help us move back and forth between the world of reality and the magic ideal world of the imagination. The importance of this is clearly recognized in children's literature, where the treehouse and the cave are paralleled by Lewis Carroll's rabbit-hole and looking glass, by H. G. Wells' door in the wall, by C. S. Lewis's wardrobe and so forth. These locations all function as gateways between the worlds. Alternatively, children's literature allows you to jump from one world to the other by clutching the talismanic object very tight and closing your eyes, while perhaps also uttering a magic formula and wishing.

More prosaically, I take all this to mean that the talismanic object works simply by its power to stimulate the production of stories. Looking for help, we have somehow come to associate resort to the talisman with a switching-on of the imagination. Once that primal mythopoeic faculty in us has been activated, life becomes bearable. Stories, remember, have the power to order chaos, reconcile conflict, solve problems, compensate for loss and inadequacy, beguile the night and defer death. So long as we can keep the stories going, our life can continue.

All this suggests an alternative reading of the anomalousness of Jesus. In the past his anomalousness was read as setting up a great cosmic value-scale. At the summit of perfection and holiness were (roughly speaking) authoritative celibate types, usually masculine and never distracted. At the bottom of the value-scale were put-upon housewives and other responsible people, always distracted and with little opportunity for being single-mindedly 'spiritual'. But on the alternative view the anomalous is ambiguous, transgressive and liberating because it is a story-catalyst. By making Jesus so anomalous the Evangelists were seeing him as questioning rather than consolidating value-scales, and were giving him a power to generate and attract myths that has lasted to the present day. He is still talismanic, for the two World Wars produced notable examples of people resorting to him *in extremis*, and the Christ-myth still provides a starting-point for new films and books of good quality.

This talismanic quality of Jesus is what theology has called his saving activity, his redemptive power. It may still work, provided we have the courage to break away from standard interpretations of him; provided that we are sufficiently bold in repudiating the old sexist and power-hungry orthodoxy and radically refictionalizing Jesus. There is no good reason why this should not be done, and therefore no reason why we should not be able to write out those features of the Gospel story – such as its sexism – that have become objectionable to the modern reader. In recent years interesting literary interpretations of Jesus have portrayed him as homosexual, heterosexual and androgynous. He has to be portrayed as a uniter of opposites, and therefore as being mixed, paradoxical and unclean in the eyes of the conventionally religious, in order to be atoning. Only one who is unclean *can* atone. To atone, he must straddle a boundary and partake of two different natures. That is why what matters about Jesus is not an orthodoxy fixed in one story, but his anomalousness, that is, his power to generate many stories for many people.[11]

5

THEOLOGICAL STORIES

(a) Ritual knowledge

The first form in which societies everywhere codify knowledge and make it the general rule is ritual. A ritual is a chain of symbolic behaviours prescribed by tradition. Everyone knows that it must be performed under certain circumstances and in the correct order, and everybody seems to know what the point of it is. At least, they don't express any puzzlement about the matter. It is so obvious to everyone that the ritual must be performed with all due ceremony that we borrow from the sphere of ritual the very vocabulary in which we say that something or other must be done rightly, duly, punctiliously, piously, observantly, decently, respectfully, precisely, methodically and religiously. This extremely rich vocabulary both bears witness to and explains the importance of rituals. For rituals teach order: the social order, the ordering of space and time, and the correct order in which tasks should be performed. In this role they are so obviously valuable that they have abundant forerunners in the animal world, especially in reproductive behaviour, and among social animals.

Rituals resemble stories. They are general and symbolic, they are temporally extended, they embody chains of actforms and they communicate socially-important knowledge. The myth-and-ritual school of historians of religion maintained indeed that all myths were originally generated by religious rituals, and at first existed in close association with them.[1] A myth was a story recounted at a religious ritual. Another indication of the intimate relationship between rituals and narratives is the way in which children's nursery tales become ritualized and drop into fixed forms of words. Naturally, the best-loved stories are admonishments: do as Mother says, respect the social order – one, two, three, big, middle, little, chair, bowl, bed – or you may find yourself getting gobbled up by a wolf, a bear, a giant or a witch.

Rituals are obliged to resemble melodies and narratives if they are to succeed in their function of inculcating the correct order and no other. A melody is so effective in making a chain of musical notes memorable that you can remember them only in the right order, and it is well-nigh impossible to get the order wrong. Poems, nursery tales and stories generally are almost as memorable. If ritual is to be as effective as melodies and stories in making a precise order memorable, then it must have running through it something analogous to the logic of plot or melody. Each step in the ritual must *lead on* to the next without fail.

This is indeed what we find: ritual has a narrative or dramatic sort of logic, and people are acutely disturbed or distressed by any failure to get the order of proceedings just right. In a famous comparison, Freud described a religion as a public obsessional neurosis and an obsessional neurosis as a private religion. He had in mind the fact that in both cases people are very anxious about the correct sequence of actions, and there is no reason to baulk at the comparison. Cultural codes have actually produced our emotions and set them in order in the first place. If it is the case that the dynamics of our emotional life were first formed by melodies, stories and rituals, then it is not surprising that misfires are painful.

However, a consequence of all this is that ritual knowledge is general and socially compulsory. It is unconcerned with the individual. When you are taking part in a ritual you are not a unique individual, but merely an instance of a universal form or pattern. You are just 'the Bride', or whatever. The world of myth and ritual is a cyclical and traditional world in which standard patterns simply go on repeating themselves. Knowledge is knowledge of an unchanging and universal order, and there is as yet no interest in individual human psychology. The gods themselves are part of this order, so that not even they have very much by way of individual personality. They are sentenced constantly to repeat themselves, for they are something like personifications of cosmic patterns and forces. They are not able to be true individuals, because in order to be an individual you must be one whose life happens only once and who does everything only once. Caught up in the eternal return of the same, the gods were not able to be as individual as a modern human person. Poor things, they were not mortal. And the ritual human being was not in much better case. She could die indeed, but because everything in her life was the return of a universal, she was personally dormant. It was difficult for her to awaken to her own mortal individuality, until she could escape from the universal.

(b) From ritual to prose fiction

In the great Bronze Age civilizations human life at first got all its meaning and value solely from its relation to endlessly-recurrent sacred archetypal patterns, beings and standards. The gods had lived on earth not very long ago, and had set all the standards for everything. When they withdrew they handed over to colleges of priests, or to the demigod kings who claimed descent from them. These stewards, whether priests or kings, who ruled on behalf of the gods had no higher aim than to maintain uncorrupted the perfect order which not long ago had been established by the gods. The pious and punctilious observance of rituals by everyone from the king downwards helped to keep present practice up to Golden Age standards. Human life had no significant future, only a past into which it continually returned; and human beings had very little subjectivity or individual self-consciousness. They existed only as 'the cattle of God' and as servants in his house. That means that they existed merely as occasions for the cyclical return of the universal.

How do we know this? Only from the character of the surviving literature and art of the second and third millennia BCE. And when did human beings like us first appear? I mean a type of human being who is conscious and self-conscious enough to know that we are on our own, that we must use our wits to survive, that life is an enigma, that suffering and death await us all in the end, that the gods must be venerated and be treated with wary respect, and that in the short run whether your life is happy or miserable depends largely on how you get on with other human beings, who are a tricky lot to understand. A human being who sees life in these terms has approximately our sort of understanding of the human condition. When did such people first appear? The only evidence we have or could have is literary. The surviving literature shows us such human beings beginning to emerge in heroic poetry, epic and saga somewhere between Gilgamesh and the Odyssey. But the literary form within which a modern selfhood is definitively constituted is prose fiction, and it is still the case that the Hebrew Bible is as early a text as any we know that contains large amounts of straight prose fiction, the supreme achievement of religious humanism.

Don't get me wrong. I am *not* saying that the Hebrew Bible offers or even could offer evidence that at some particular time in the past people became subjectively self-conscious in the sense of having a private space of selfhood inside them. That is an occultist notion, and we have already repudiated it. One must stick to the text, and not postulate anything outside it. Instead I want to define prose fiction's new sort of selfhood simply in terms of what goes on in the text. It is this: in prose fiction the human person as a character in the story is individuated in and through his 'horizontal' interactions with other persons. The narrative reveals and develops human character by describing the dynamics of human social relations. That means, in particular, conversational exchanges. What is new and wonderful here is that the particular, the merely human, the only-once, has become interesting. In the older mythical-ritual texts you were constituted a human being only through your relation to the universal that once again realized itself in you. The contingent human as such was not important. You got your value from being taken up into the re-iterating divine life. But the Hebrew Bible astonishes the reader because even in some of its earliest texts (such as the court history of King David) and oldest traditions (such as the narratives in Genesis) the writers are using the techniques not of myth, but of secular humanist fiction. They call upon, not the stylized categories of mythical thinking, but the psychological cunning of the fiction-writer. True, they remain very insistent upon archaic theological themes, such as the hidden ways in which Providence works to secure the continuation of the sacred line. But they nevertheless treat such themes in and through a close attention to psychological detail, communicated by narrative art. Indeed, just by its use of prose rather than epic poetry the Bible itself in its sagas and historical narratives is already beginning the radical humanization of religion.[2]

What does this mean? It means that prose fiction as a literary form knows no other persons than human persons. All life is low life. The world has become radically human and relational, and a person simply *is* her or his exchanges with other human persons. In prose fiction the real world is just the human world, and the human person is not a spiritual substance in a house of clay, but simply coincides with his or her own life among others.

This world of prose fiction that we find in the patriarchal narratives in Genesis, and in I and II Samuel, is a world made entirely of human behaviours and communications. People have often commented on how secular it seems. The same is true also of the world of Jesus' parables, in which neither God nor any supernatural apparatus appears. In what ways then can God enter into the purely humanist world of biblical prose fiction? He may be a brooding presence off-stage, guiding the action in a hidden way; but such a suggestion raises the interesting question of how in that case we can tell the difference between God and the author, who is also transcendental, off the page and manipulating events. Secondly, there may be an indirect or negative presence of God in the narrative by way of people's religious beliefs and experiences, and what the narrative's treatment of them seem to suggest about prophecy, about the psychology of religion and so forth. But the narrative gives us and can give us only the varieties of human religiousness. It cannot deliver the religious object in person.

Or can it? – the third possibility is that God may intervene and become a character in the story. But in that case he has to become a human being. For fiction is, we said, entirely about human actions and relationships. Animals, extra-terrestrials and demons who want to get into the story and contribute to the action must become human to do so. Similarly, God in the Old Testament stories can get in only by way of being masculine, talking correct period Hebrew, sharing the general assumptions of the age, having human-type emotions and intentions, and behaving in general like an extra-powerful and demanding king. God simply cannot get in at all, except upon these very stringent conditions.

Roughly, *myth* is able to be about the gods because mere human beings have not yet fully arrived upon the scene. It pictures a world in which we live only through the gods. *Epic* poetry gives us a mixed, battling world of heroes, demigods, monsters and the like. The world of *fiction* is purely human. All three genres can be found in the Bible. But it is the fiction that is new and extraordinary.

(c) Christian epic theology

In spite of Jesus' parables and sayings, Christianity at first chose not to build upon the Bible's prose-fiction, humanistic tradition. The paradoxical consequence was that for a very long period Christian faith was less humanistic than Jewish. Perhaps it is in the canvasses of Rembrandt that we can best see Christianity belatedly catching up with the mother-faith.

Earlier, though, the main intellectual effort had been put into epic narrative theology. This enterprise was launched by Paul, and was much influenced by the exigencies of Jewish-Christian controversy. Paul was battling to defend Jesus' messiahship, to explain the sacrificial significance of his death, and to legitimate the claim of the church to be 'the new Israel'. This required him to attempt a re-reading of the whole biblical tradition. Balancing Christ against figures such as Adam and Moses, he set up a series of binary oppositions: Fall and Redemption, Old Covenant and New Covenant, promise and fulfilment, law and gospel, sin and grace, carnal and spiritual. Around such oppositions he began to weave a huge epic theological narrative. Amongst other things, it had to explain the present religious status of the continuing Jewish Synagogue. Why had God chosen to fulfil his promises to his own chosen people in a manner which the majority of them could not or would not recognize? And where did they stand now? Was God unjust, were they outcast, and might they in the end yield?[3]

All these concerns gave to Christian epic narrative theology its characteristic flavour. It is of cosmic scale, stretching from the creation of the angels to the final bliss after the General Judgment. It is trying to exhibit in the whole story the workings of a just, wise and benevolent Providence. It is very much concerned with legitimacy, the legitimacy of Christ as the Messiah and of his church as the inheritor of God's promises, and the legitimacy of Paul himself and also, by extension, of other teachers and rulers within the church. It is concerned about the origin of evil, seeking to show us how God is working to vanquish it and why we can be sure of the final triumph of the good. And finally it has a hidden Other against whom the whole thing was originally developed as a polemic, namely the Jew who refuses to acknowledge Jesus' messiahship.

In many of the greatest European cathedrals there is a pair of carved stone figures representing the church and the synagogue. They are usually portrayed as two young women, sisters, equally beautiful and even (as at Bamberg) sensual. But the synagogue is blindfolded. One wants to ask: 'Who put on that blindfold, and why?'

The concern for legitimacy and the anti-Jewish motivation of the old theological epic combined to give it a dogmatic and even ideological flavour. It was after all teaching that we are right and the other lot are wrong. Furthermore, until the rise of critical history the history of salvation was sincerely believed to be just the plain Truth. Only very recently have we felt free to regard it as a work of art and to enjoy at least some versions of it pretty much as we enjoy the epic works of Dante, Milton, Blake and Joyce.[4]

When we thus consider the Christian epic aesthetically, a few points about it strike us forcefully. It is clearly very remote and strange in its view of the world. It was also prodigiously complex and many-levelled, fighting a number of different battles on different fronts. It was at once an interpretation of scripture, a proof of ecclesiastical legitimacy, a refutation of Judaism, a pocket encyclopaedia of world history, a vindication of God, an allegory of the progress of the soul, a moral fable, and much else besides. Unfortunately, after the linguistic levelling-down imposed by the rise of early modern science people began to lose the ability to handle such literary complexities, and after the rise of critical history they could no longer accept epic grand narrative so innocently as before.

There is a further difficulty: Christian epic combines great literary complexity with an uncomfortably essentialist and uniform account of human beings and human nature. It is as if the God's-eye view sees human beings from such a great height that they all look the same. One standard doctrine of 'man', of sin, of justification, of sanctification and the rest of it applies to everyone. We are back in a thought-world in which only the universal is important. Individual differences between people are not of religious interest.

They are nowadays, though. We live in a prose-fiction world in which everybody is different because everybody is assigned a quite different role by the text. And, to extend the metaphor, there are now many, many texts offering us different parts to play. What is religiously-interesting about a person in our world is not the common nature that she shares with every other human being who has ever lived, but the respects in which the role she plays is unique and unlike anyone else's. For us epic narrative theology may be aesthetically moving, but it does not speak to our personal condition. Not in the least. We need the humanistic sort of religion which completely rejects standardization, has no orthodoxy, and rejoices in difference. Its development is long overdue.

The historic turning-point can be seen in *Paradise Lost*. Milton lived just at the time when epic was ending and fiction arriving. To write a convincing early-modern epic theodicy, he had to create fictional figures with whom the reader could identify. Unfortunately, all the virtuous characters – Adam and Eve before the Fall, the Angels, Christ and so on – came to him readymade from tradition, and as a result they are dull stereotypes. Satan, on the other hand, has appetites, desires and idiosyncrasies. He moves the action along, and we readily identify with him. Milton's misfortune, and the neat paradox for us to note, is that Satan is the most real character because he is the most freshly-fictioned. And so it now is with us and our world.

(d) But who is the narrator?

In all texts a game is played between author and reader. Even the dullest treatise needs to employ, and cannot help but employ, rhetorical and narrative techniques. The author must plan to interest the reader; he has to bring on his cast of ideas in a certain order, move them around persuasively, and generally put on a good performance. Even the most abstract prose is a puppet-show, a narrative entertainment managed by a concealed showman. The showman-author has to pique and to *lead on* the reader, an idiom implying that a seduction is taking place.

Such hidden artifice reaches its highest pitch of complexity in fiction. The text describes a social world of which neither the author nor the reader are inhabitants. How do we gain access to this imaginary world, and from what point of view do we see it? The author has to devise a reporter, who is able to see into the world of the fiction in a certain way and from a certain viewpoint. The whole text is then written as by the reporter, who observes the events and narrates the story. This observer is very often a marginal character, who sees, hears, speculates and generally watches to see what will happen, but does not take much part. She is proxy for the reader, her task being only to give the reader an eye to see the action with. The author is in control, and the narrator is self-effacing. Alternatively the narrator may be the leading actor, in which case the author will be self-effacing, and the book will be couched in the form of an autobiography, like *Jane Eyre*.

Both these narrators are what the Germans call 'I-persons' (*Ich-Personen*). Their closest cinematic parallel is the case where the field of view of the camera exactly coincides with the visual field of a leading character, perhaps a man on the run. But in the case of the cinema it has been found that the convention of sticking strictly to looking through one person's eyes is too restrictive. Audiences prefer to stand a little apart from the character with whom they are identifying. So the film may be made as if it were a partial biography of its leading character, who is seen from outside. We follow her fortunes: the sequences are so constructed that we see everything in terms of how it affects her. We know, hear, see what she knows, hears, sees. The film may also incorporate scenes at which she is not present, from which we pick up some vital pieces of information that remain unknown to her. We may learn for instance that she is in danger. There is certainly a strong temptation to introduce such scenes, because they greatly excite the audience. We feel anxiety on the heroine's behalf, but also pleasure in having the advantage over her. It is strange, more than a little perverse, and a well-known fact that a touch of distance or dramatic irony actually heightens arousal. But the use of such techniques raises questions about the status of the narrator, who is beginning to acquire superhuman knowledge. He slips out of the action and becomes instead its puppeteer, manipulating events. And us, too.

The next step is to make the narrator plural. The narrative still limits itself to the human point of view and to what the various characters in the story can observe or know, but it moves around from one character's viewpoint to another's. The impression of a dialectical-humanist or interactive social world is thus created, with many possibilities for dramatic irony and subtlety of plotting.

Discussing these matters, Roland Barthes points out that we do not need to postulate either an author or a reader outside the text.[5] This is convenient, because many kinds of oral and traditional literature – legends, folk-tales, myths and so forth – are authorless. We don't know, and it scarcely even matters, who first composed them or for what audience. In the case of a modern literary work, the point Barthes is making is that by the way it is constructed the text itself will show sufficiently who is the narrator giving it and who is the recipient reading it. The clearest and most vivid illustration of this point is the epistolary novel which consists entirely of an exchange of letters. At each point in the text both a sender and a receiver are being projected. Barthes is saying that every text is like that: it has to posit somewhere that it is coming from, and it has to posit an audience to whom it is addressed. This positing is internal, because both the narrator and the addressee are literary constructs, fictions fully immanent within the text.

What about the author, the writer of the text, whom Barthes is so keen to play down? Even in the epistolary novel, where the author would seem to be most completely hidden, it is arguable that she is nevertheless still immanent. We are after all reading both sides of a private correspondence, gathered together and arranged in order for us. Transcendentally, the author is presupposed as the agency that has produced this synthesis and is managing the reader's experience. B.S. Johnson took matters a stage further by producing a novel which consisted of twelve separate fascicles randomly packed in a red box. You the reader were supposed to go through them in any order you chose. But even in this case there was still a single literary work, and an author was therefore presupposed. The old analogy between the author/book relation and the God/world relation is curiously difficult to escape. Literary modernism keeps trying to get away from it, and keeps finding that it is still stuck with it.

Even more strangely, there is also paradox at the opposite extreme, because the literary traditionalism that wants to affirm the godlike author and the theological character of imaginative writing *also* runs into acute problems. In prose fiction the extreme case of this is also the most familiar: the omniscient narrator, who seems to have free and unrestricted access to the doings and the undisclosed thoughts and intentions of all and every one of the characters. The action is seen as it were from a God's-eye view, so that in the narrator's relation to events there is a certain predestinarianism. At the opening of the story the narrator already knows in full the tale he plans to tell: it is all in the past tense, it has all already happened. The narrator is certainly not going to be surprised, but he would like to create surprise. His chief problems then are technical: he will want to organize his story in such a way as most effectively to entertain and edify the reader.

I suspect that the reason why the omniscient narrator was the norm in traditional literature is that his authority was, precisely, that of tradition itself. Tradition always represents itself as complete and omnicompetent. However, enough has been said by now to indicate that in all forms of narrative writing the questions of the narrator's exact status and knowledge, and of the way in which the narrative's impact upon the reader is designed and angled, are very important. These questions are transcendental, in the sense that the answers to them are not incorporated in the text, but are throughout presupposed by the text. To answer questions about the narrator we must look at where the text presents itself as coming from.

Now, as we have emphasized, much of scripture and much of theology is expressly narrative in form. It has been penned by human authors, and there has been much scholarly discussion of their sources, methods and theological motives. There has been very much less discussion of the ways in which God is placed and his role in the narrative is managed, and almost none of the relation between the narrator and God. Who is the narrator of theology, and where has he got the story from? In autobiographical religious writing – testimony, confession, apologia – it is clear that the narrator is the author in person, an ordinary human subject directly confessing her own life-history, religious experiences and feelings. Such a first-person narrator may also be found in scripture, for example in many Psalms. But in all formal theological writing an extremely grand and magisterial omniscient narrator has always been employed. *Who is he?* He is careful never to say, but this is the archetypal occurrence of his voice:

> In the beginning God created the heaven and the earth. And the earth was without form and void; and darkness was upon the face of the deep. And the Spirit of God moved upon the face of the waters. And God said, Let there be light: and there was light.

Who's talking? Where does this text present itself as coming from? Every narrative must have a narrator who tells the tale from a certain standpoint, but the standpoint from which these sentences purport to emanate is one that the narrative itself assures us does not exist and could not exist. Nobody senior to God could have been around, ready and waiting to watch him make the world, and we have no idea what it could have been for someone actually to hear God say, 'Let there be light'. A similar problem arises in relation to all those modern works of popular science which describe the Big Bang and the evolution of the early universe, from an imagined narrator's viewpoint outside it and anterior to it. There is and there can be no such standpoint. At least, the theory described from the standpoint says there is no such standpoint, which appears to make the text self-refuting. The same problem arises in the text of a great dogmatic theologian such as Karl Barth. Much or most of Barth's text is written from the point of view of an impossible, super-omniscient narrator who within his narrative creates God as a character and moves him around, making God a player in a drama he is staging for us. But who can this narrator be, who is in a position to direct God's performance in the narrative, and to report to us on what God is planning and getting up to? Obviously the literary form of Barth's text is in flagrant contradiction with the message that it is purporting to deliver – and so it has always been since the very beginning of theology. God cannot be written about at all except in some form of narrative mode, and theologians have always been aware of an unavoidable resulting tendency to anthropomorphize God. To write a story in which God is a character, one must give God a gender, a script, emotions and dispositions. Obvious enough. But the problem of the narrator is even more serious. Where is he coming from, what is his standpoint and *how does he get the authority to script and direct God's performance?* There can be no satisfactory answer.

The difficulty arose in the first place because scripture-writers and theologians were not content with the personal and confessional style of religious writing. It was only expressive. It lacked compelling authority. To beef up your religious writing, to give it grandeur, objectivity and authority, the I-person who uttered religious confession and testimony was replaced by an updated version of the old impersonal and omniscient narrator of myth.

Unfortunately, the doctrine of God expounded *in* the text leaves nothing for the omniscient narrator *of* the text to be. There is nowhere for what he says to be coming from.

Thus formal theological writing fails in its attempt to transcend the merely personal expressiveness of religious writing, as we acknowledge when for example, we speak of 'Calvinism'. Calvin was certainly not trying merely to create an -ism called Calvinism. He is trying to persuade us that things are thus and so with God absolutely. Many of his texts are admittedly personal and controversial. In others, however, he certainly does adopt the grand manner, and must do so if he is to go beyond merely reporting what is in scripture and what he, Calvin, thinks. But when the grand manner is assumed and the text reports absolutely on what God is up to, the God of whom the text speaks is already omni-everything and unsurpassable in all directions, so who is the omniscient narrator? Alas, only Calvin himself, putting on rhetorical airs. So the world has decided that after all he has managed only to invent 'Calvinism'.

The sheer magnitude of the omniscient-narrator problem was first pointed out by Kierkegaard, especially in relation to Hegel's philosophy. In speaking of himself as a 'poet' and a person 'without authority', Kierkegaard was in effect saying that it is folly to adopt a literary pretence that we can altogether transcend our human viewpoint, and that the grand objective dogmatic manner should therefore be given up. In any case, what is wrong with personal, confessional religious writing and existential or literary philosophy? Their only defect is that they don't assume a right to lord it over other people. Calvin's impersonal omniscient narrator was a deception, masking nothing but Calvin's own will-to-power.

Can dogmatic theology be saved from this line of criticism? I think not. The omniscient-narrator problem could not be recognized in its full gravity before the rise of literary philosophy – that is, before the nineteenth century. But so far as the problem was recognized at all, it was thought to be disposed of by a near-identification of the omniscient narrator with God himself. This would seem to be the meaning of the orthodox Catholic and Protestant belief that the scriptures 'have God for their author'.

Nobody ever doubted that human penmen physically wrote down the text, so that ascribing its 'authorship' to God must have been a way of saying that God himself supplies the standpoint for and 'authorizes' (literally) the narrator whose voice is heard in the text.

The argument for this is as follows: if you pointed out to a pre-modern theologian that by definition there is no standpoint from which any narrator might have observed God creating the world, and that therefore the statement that *God said 'Let there be light'* is self-stultifying, you would surely have received the reply that at all events God himself was around at the moment of the world's first creation, and God inspired the human penman who composed the Genesis account of creation. So the penman was 'authorized' by God to rise to the grand, objective manner of reporting the event. God's direct inspiration justifies the assumption by the text of the omniscient-narrator mode.

Oddly, this is no reply at all. Remember, the omniscient narrator is only a fictioned standpoint from which another fiction (a story about God's doings) can supposedly issue. I pointed out that there is a special kind of contradiction between these two fictions, which makes the text very queerly self-stultifying. The reply that God inspired the penman to write a special kind of nonsense cannot make it one whit the less nonsensical. It certainly doesn't show how God could ever exist *outside* stories. And there remains something very odd about a revelation of God in a text in which his performance as an agent in a story is stage-managed from an impossible fictioned standpoint. Can God really cease to coincide with himself, objectify himself, and write about himself as it were from the outside? The claim seems to be that if the sacred writers were to write truly about God, God just *had* to set up for them a fictional standpoint from which he could be written about in the third person, as a character. The narrator scripts God's words, explains his motivations and controls his acts – as, for example, in the book of Job. Subsequent theology has continued to avail itself of the same standpoint – but it is still an impossible standpoint. Why is all this done?

It is done, as the assumption of an impersonal narrative mode is always done, in an attempt to transcend the subjectivity of the speaker and achieve a grand, objective, authoritative type of discourse. Scientists do it, lawyers do it, historians do it. They mean to say: 'This is not merely my personal opinion: it's Truth, it's how things are, it is the Law'. As we have seen though, it cannot work – at least, not quite in the way intended. Theology stays narrative. God is produced within narrative, and the fiction of an authoritative omniscient narrator who tells us the whole Truth about God not merely fails to hike God out of narrative and into objectivity, but is itself absurd anyway. Our language about God does not become 'scientific' or dogmatic. It remains expressive and fictional. Thus, doctrinal talk about 'what God has done' cannot help but be situated on the sort of fictioned-past timescale that is conjured up by phrases like 'In the beginning', 'Once upon a time' and 'In those days'. Not that there is anything wrong with such talk: while it cheerfully admits its own merely human, fictional, 'non-realist' status, it is fine; but when it starts claiming more than that it makes itself absurd.

What follows?

(e) Fictional theology

The sort of theology that is written as if by an omniscient narrator has a great deal wrong with it. It suffers from a queer kind of incoherence, for according to the content of what it teaches the literary form in which it conveys the teaching is impossible. That is, if there really does exist outside the text and prior to it the infinite and holy God that dogmatic theology postulates, then there can be no standpoint for writing about him in the way it does. Nobody can be in a position to look down upon God, to watch God, or make him into a character in a story. So the omniscient narrator as a literary device fails to give to theological writing the assured extra-textual objectivity that it hankers after. This failure is, however, no matter for regret. For the real interest of such would-be objective theo- logical writing was in any case not in the religious liberation of human beings, but merely in the validation of some earthly authority's religious power and control over them. The difference here is quite straightforward, and I have been stating it for years: realist theologies follow the historic church in saying that man was made for religion, whereas non-realist theologies follow Jesus in saying (Mark 2. 27) that religion was made for man.

The end of the Grand-Narrative type of dogmatic theology clears the way for a different sort of theological writing, which I shall call simply fictional. This is not so novel as you might think. By general consent, at least some biblical books present their teachings in the form of straight prose fiction. Ruth, Jonah and Esther are obvious examples, while the Apocrypha adds Susannah, Judith, Tobit and Bel and the Dragon. Many biblical books also contain at least some expressly fictional material such as the parables of Jesus, and indeed in post-biblical times the rabbis made very extensive use of stories, legends and parables in their narrative *midrashim*. Christianity too developed a large popular literature of apocryphal gospels, lives of the saints and so forth.

It is extraordinary that one should need to say such a thing, but is it not obvious that the very prominence of fictional narrative in our religious tradition – and still more the fact that we often cannot tell for sure, and it doesn't matter at all anyway, whether a particular biblical book is fiction or not – shows that religion is a communal human imaginative creation, and shows it so clearly that the only question is why people should ever have supposed otherwise?

If we set aside the big theological names (whom few in fact can have read), we can see early Christianity as having been grounded in popular literature and storytelling. Because of this, mediaeval culture eventually became highly visual and narrative. The distinction between history and fiction was blurred, to put it mildly. People were simply not anxious about the distinction between God's own true and real Story of things, as written in scripture and acted out in world history, and all the other stories, which have been produced merely by the human imagination. No doubt the chief reason why the mediaevals were not too worried about the history-fiction distinction is that they remained so confident in their underlying objectivism and rationalism. That is, they still took it for granted that the human artist and craftsman at work was tracking and re-presenting heavenly and archetypal patterns. The mediaeval imagination was allegorical: everything drew its reality from the eternal order of which it was an illustration. Thus there was no realism or naturalism in the modern sense. Artists did not originate, but merely portrayed or represented. They did not know of any other way to work, because they did not have any very developed conception of independent human creativity. There was no question of breaking away from or rivalling God, and writers were on the whole content to see themselves as recycling traditional plots and themes. It was still a matter of course that God's creativity was primary and human creativity was secondary. God was archetypal and we were ectypal.

While God thus continued to inspire and to form all human creativity, it could present no threat to him, and medieval culture could continue to take a decidedly relaxed view of the human production of religious images and fictions. But all this comes to an abrupt end with Protestantism. There is a sudden wave of intense anxiety that the human creative imagination may be about to break away from God, and there is therefore a severe clampdown on visual imagery and fiction. Fiercely rationalistic, Protestantism sets about giving images, rituals, legends and fictions a bad name. It attempts to inhibit the free play of the literary imagination, and to bind the believer very closely to the letter of scripture When there is only one story, and that a story not written by human beings at all but by God alone, then it is as if there are no stories. The world is fictionless: there is only the plain dogmatic Truth of things, absolute and unrivalled.

In Protestantism the absolute sovereignty of God's Will thus comes to be affirmed by way of a vehement attack upon images and fictions, somewhat as in classical philosophy Logos or objective Reason was affirmed by way of a satirical attack upon Muthos. But this time the assault upon the merely human is more severe. To ensure that there shall be no return to mediaeval permissiveness, the Analogy of Being is denied. This means that things human no longer in the old way participate in things divine, and the human artist therefore can no longer draw upon archetypal divine patterns. The effects of all this have been far-reaching. In its anxiety to secure social discipline and God's absolute monarchy, Protestantism in effect secularized the human mind by depriving it of its old natural, creaturely community with the divine mind. Our ability to generate images, metaphors and stories was now something suspect, because merely human. It might easily be regarded as the result of Satan's influence. At any rate, Protestantism sowed in believers a deep suspicion of the visual arts, the stage and the novel. All of them are seen as encouraging rebellious or lustful fantasies. So Protestantism tried to secure discipline by requiring the renunciation of our potentially wayward creative and imaginative powers.

In attacking imagery Protestantism was also attacking everything that is contaminated by metaphoricity, mediacy and secondariness. That includes all metaphorical, fictional and rhetorical uses of language. In sharp contrast to merely human literature, Protestantism portrays God's utterance in scripture as being completely direct and controlled, and never wandering; that is, it is inerrant. God's word is not in any way oblique; it is as straight as a sword. What he has written cannot slip, slide or decay, but is 'literally' true. So Protestantism actually seeks to deny fictionality in scripture, and tries to defend the 'literal historicity' of books like Daniel and Jonah. Indeed, the Protestant ideology of the Bible has been so intense and exigent that for centuries it has altogether blinded people to the Bible's manifest literary character, as was eloquently pointed out by S.T. Coleridge and Matthew Arnold in the last century.[6] People have been dominated by a highly *anti*-literary 'literalism' which can still lead them to insist upon the literal historicity of, for example, the miracles associated with Jesus. In the name of the Bible people have insisted upon a far more dogmatic or propositional kind of faith than is required in the Bible.

Such people now sound, however, somewhat out of date. For in recent generations our world has increasingly become visual and fictionalist once more. This time our stained-glass windows are cinema and video screens, with moving pictures. Our culture is in many ways popular-mediaeval: think of our astrology, fringe medicine, cartoons, witchcraft, science-fiction, cult-figures, commercial logos and so forth. What we lack is the old metaphysical underpinning; but the effect of this lack is only to make the culture even more profoundly fictionalist than it was in the Middle Ages.

To turn theology in the same direction we need to undo a whole series of ideological distinctions – between divine revelation and human imagination, literal and metaphorical, truth and fiction, fact and interpretation, history and myth, revealed truth and the 'earthen vessels' in which it is conveyed, surface and depth, unchanging core-truth and its changing vestures. And indeed it is precisely these distinctions that have been breaking down in recent years.

Since, however, the old belief in objective 'literal' truth is not dead yet, we need new arguments to prove the religious superiority of fictitious religion. Here are some.

First, the analogy with ethics. In traditional society moral values were built into enduring social institutions, and summarized in authoritative codes of religious law. Respect for an objective moral order even appeared to be built into human nature. But modern society is too critical, too reflective, too narrative and too much aware of human diversity and historical change. The old machinery for guarding and transmitting values just won't work any more. Our whole culture has come to be based upon the criticism of tradition, the questioning of authority, and the cultivation of a due respect for the diversity of human beings and the mixed character of human motives and life-situations. Our modern intellectual virtues therefore cannot help but undermine our traditional moral institutions. So we need a new sort of ethics, appropriate to the sort of culture we now have. In our present type of culture moral values cannot be fixed, codified or held unchanged. Strangely, our moral values now seem to be desperately ephemeral, elusive and ambiguous. We cannot keep them still. We find that they must be continually reimagined or refictioned. Ethics has therefore to take the new form of a continual activity of criticizing the existing moral

order and recreating our values. For their vitality and effective-
ness, values depend upon metaphors, and metaphors can grow
stale. Our values therefore need to be scrutinized, reminted and
refreshed in narratives, films and plays. The moral tradition has
to be kept alive by an unceasing aesthetic work of criticism and
recreation. We must revolutionize it to maintain it. So we have
now a fictionalist ethic. True, it is not the same as the old
objectivist ethic. It is different. But it is just as serious, just as
much an ethic, and I think it works rather well. We would be
perfectly satisfied with it, if only our judgment were not clouded
by futile nostalgia for the old order.

By analogy, all the same things are true of religion. It too has
to be continually criticized and refictioned, or it dies. The classic
warning is the fate of fundamentalism, which attempts to fix
religion and hold it still, and as a result has almost destroyed
religion. Fundamentalism is religion that is imaginatively dead
and therefore is not religion at all, which shows that the storyteller's imagination is necessary to the life of religion. That is,
religion lives only while we are making it up, while our
imaginations are firing and we are generating new angles, new
narratives and new metaphors. Like Jesus and the Buddha, the
classic religious teacher is not a codifier or a book-writer. The
classic teacher uses the spoken word, teaching only for the
moment, and using riddles, proverbs and parables. The teacher
creates special effects by using rhetorical devices. These tricks
work on us to kindle our imaginations, make us question the
way we evaluate ourselves, life and other people, and inspire the
creation of new values. But they are only human rhetorical
devices, and religion resembles art in being a human creative
activity whereby a certain quality of life is produced. You, you,
you have got to fiction it, because unless your own creative
imagination is engaged you cannot get your religion right.

The second argument for fictionalism draws an analogy
between religion and sex. In both cases, the needs, the fears, the
passions and the sensitivities involved are exceedingly strong.
Things can get out of control. It is vital to maintain a certain
playfulness or levity. So culture wisely makes sex into a game or
a comedy in which we are aware, sometimes of acting out

socially-preordained roles, and sometimes of ourselves devising scenarios and acting them out. We make elaborate rituals out of our courtship, etiquette, formalities, flirtations, dancing and so forth. Thus we civilize sex by making a frivolous game of it. This paradoxically enhances the fun, because sex is a form of symbolic communication. Conversely, where sex is not held at the level of a game, where it becomes symbolically impoverished and inarticulate – then it soon becomes heavy, clumsy, violent and sometimes oppressive. Especially to women.

So the argument is that frivolous, fictionalized sex is better sex, because moralized, more human, more communicative, symbolically richer. And by the same token religion too needs to be held at the level of a game, kept light, fictional and symbolically rich. Self-mocking even, because religion that is not reflectively aware of its own fictionality quickly becomes too serious, and therefore clumsy, violent and oppressive.

In this connection, we should also grasp the point that because fiction is the humanist medium, fictionalist religion is humanist religion. This is manifest in the biblical and apocryphal books already mentioned—Ruth, Jonah, Esther, Judith, Tobit, Susannah. Consider their titles: human proper names, four women and two men. In fact, this is the only group of books in the Bible in which women get a chance. They are humanist books because they are fictional; that is, the sacred is not too crushingly real and heavy. T.S. Eliot's absurd platitude to the effect that humankind cannot bear very much reality is actually true! We don't want too much reality, and we should not have it. The human world is a world of difference, plurality, perspectives, ambiguity, play, squabbles, surfaces, mockery – in short, a fictional world. Too much of the Same, the Real and the True simply snuffs it out. Metaphysics is anti-human.

Long-established binary oppositions in the culture have in the past given superior value to the deep rather than the superficial, the weighty and serious rather than the frivolous and light-hearted, the natural rather than the artificial, and the real rather than the fictional. But I say that all those value scalings need to be reversed, and I'm quoting the case of sex in the hope of persuading you. For surely everyone can recognize that to moralize and humanize sex, to make it communicatively rich, you have to make comedy of it. It has to be held at the level of a game. Frivolity, artifice and playacting are more substantial and fulfilling than is mere stupid seriousnessness.

The same is true of religion, which so-to-say comically transcends itself when it knows it is only a game. When the stories can all be told in new ways to teach new lessons, the spirit of religion can remain alive. Self-mockery saves it from literalism, and keeps it open to change. At the opposite extreme, we note that the more dogmatic and the more realistic a system of religious belief becomes, the more it becomes a system of oppression. But religious oppression, as everyone knows, is the worst kind of oppression known to humanity because it is the most inward and searching so that you can never shake it off entirely. It easily can, and often does, scar people for life. Religion needs checks on itself, so that it can remain lightweight.

The third argument is the argument from Zen. One of the most perfect of all religious traditions, Zen pursues Enlightenment through a sustained critique of religion. In the West many people pursue Truth because they want to make an idol or fetish of it, and no doubt because they believe that the possession of Truth will give them a right to exercise power over others. But Zen stories repeatedly criticize religious objectification and authoritarianism. In a word, Zen shows how fictionalist religion is true religion by being anti-religion. Try the following pun: *it sends itself up*, soars by self-mockery.

In philosophy, Zen teaching is somewhere between phenomenalism and subjective idealism. Nothing exists outside the subject-object relation, that is, outside conscious experience. However, we should not suppose that this doctrine is 'true'. It is taught only for the sake of spirituality. For Enlightenment is reached by unlearning, all the way down to nothingness:

> Subhuti was the Buddha's disciple. He was able to under-stand the potency of emptiness, the viewpoint that nothing exists except in its relationship to subjectivity and objectivity.
> One day Subhuti, in a mood of sublime emptiness, was sitting under a tree. Flowers began to fall about him.

'We are praising you for your discourse on emptiness,' the gods whispered to him.

'But I have not spoken of emptiness,' said Subhuti.

'You have not spoken of emptiness, we have not heard emptiness,' responded the gods. 'This is the true emptiness.' And blossoms showered on Subhuti as rain.[7]

Zen turns to stories and to riddles in order to avoid the paradoxes of reflexivity. In a dream Kyozan goes to Heaven, where he recognizes himself sitting in the third seat of the abode of Maitreya. He is called upon to preach. He gets up, bangs the gavel, and says: 'The truth of Mahayana teaching is transcendent; above words and thought. Do you understand?' End of sermon. Mumon, commenting on this, asks: 'Did he preach or did he not?'[8] So the story about Kyozan, dreaming of himself preaching that the truth is ineffable, is embedded in a framing story about Mumon pointing out the fact that someone who names, in words, a truth that he says cannot be put into words, seems in danger of refuting himself. For we can ask the question: 'Has he succeeded in saying what he set out to say?' – and a paradox arises. If he has succeeded in conveying the message that the truth cannot be put into words, then he must have indicated what it is that cannot be put into words, and so he has refuted himself. Yet if he has tried but has failed to convey the truth that truth is ineffable, he is also lost, for he must have spoken falsely and have misrepresented the truth. He would have done better to keep his mouth shut. And Zen leaves it at that, because Enlightenment does not come about as a result of any positive teaching. Enlightenment is not a doctrine but a cure for humankind's oldest and most paradoxical illusions. You cannot even spell out clearly what these illusions are, because there is nowhere and nothing for them to be; so you cannot spell out what the cure is either. Which is why Zen is communicated in riddles and stories. Riddles and stories can show what dogmatic teaching cannot directly say. By which I mean only that whereas the dogmatic assertion, 'The truth cannot be put into words' is reflexively paradoxical *even in heaven*,[9] in the example just given Mumon's question, 'Did he preach or did he not?' makes the point successfully without itself falling into paradox. Where dogma fails, the riddle can win.

Translating this into Western terms, fictionalist Christianity is not a doctrine but an anti-doctrine. Our religious problem is that we are discontented. We cannot reconcile ourselves to the flux of appearances, the transience of life and the approach of death. We dream of an impossible Beyond in which we will find certain Truth, eternal happiness, absolute reality. The task of religion is not to gratify this incoherent yearning, but to cure us of it by telling us stories. The moral of all Christian stories is: 'Give up those illusory mystical yearnings, accept the human condition, love your neighbour, pour your own life out into the common life of all humanity. In a word, give up God and be content with Christ.'

However, if it is put as bluntly as that people will of course not accept it. So the story-teller's art is needed.

6

STORY ANTI-STORY

(a) Zen also refutes itself

Zen is undoubtedly clever. It is religion – anti-religion pursuing its path to religious awakening (*satori*) by deliberately renouncing almost everything that people in the West seek from religion – objective reality, guarantees, authority, consoling myths. Instead Zen aims to precipitate the student suddenly into the truth of universal emptiness, the insubstantiality and lack of any permanent identity that pervades everything, and the failure therefore of words to latch on to any reality.

Zen itself recognizes in story after story the paradox of trying to use language to speak of or gesture towards an un-thing outside language before which language fails. Like other Eastern religions it dreams of escape. The escape from textuality, the world that language conjures up, is enlightenment. But how within text can I specify what it is to 'escape' from text? There is no way 'out' of a chain of written signs like this one. It is linear and unidirectional. Each sign relates only to the others that come before and after it, and none jumps out of the row altogether. Furthermore, what we are trying to escape to is supposed to be a non-narrative realm of timeless, changeless silence and emptiness – but stories of escape are still stories. You can't narrate yourself out of the world of narrative. Wherever you narrate yourself to is thereby incorporated within the world of stories.

In the Middle East and the West believers seek to go beyond language to a God who altogether transcends language and is more real than words can tell. He is, as it were, too massively solid for mere weak slippery ambiguous words to compass him.

So the last two sentences have been self-refuting. I can't have written them. Queer, but in Zen the ambition is even queerer: it is to escape from language into the silent, empty Void that supposedly lies outside language. But *nothingness, emptiness, silence, the Void* and *outside* are also just words that have their uses within language. So too is *escape.* So how can we express what it is that Zen is trying to do, and where it is trying to go?

The special difficulty of the Zen position – and perhaps the special difficulty of Buddhism generally – is that it has to claim that language is not outsideless, period, which would make all thoughts of escape absurd, but really does have an outside to which the enlightened have gone. But what way could there be of spelling out the difference between simple outsidelessness and an ineffable outside?

Try again. Zen must maintain that there is a significant difference between two views.

On the first view, language is outsideless. There is no meaning in the attempt to escape language. We never come to the edge or to the end of language. Like the Universe in modern cosmology, the world of signs is finite but unbounded. We should therefore not be led astray by talk of seeking salvation outside language. There is no thinking, no movement and no life for us humans except within narrativity, the storylike temporally-extended movement of signs. We should be content to stay within it, because we have no alternative to doing so.

On the second view, our salvation does lie outside language. Of course we cannot *say* what is outside language, nor even think it. Admittedly there is no thing outside language. Admittedly, there is nothing outside language. But there is the Void outside language, there is Nirvana outside language, and those who have attained Enlightenment and are gone are in a state outside language. All that said, it is of course clear that the last five sentences have been paradoxical. So we now must become silent, empty and wordless. Do not even think. By being silent and empty ourselves we may be able to show what cannot be said.

I am saying that for Zen to get off the ground, there's got to be a genuine difference between the first of these views and the second. There's got to be a difference between a human situation that is radically immanent and outsideless, and a human situation that has a completely ineffable outside. How can a Zen master show us that difference? It must be demonstrable in some way, must it not, but how can it be demonstrated? How can I show, or rather, spell out, the difference between an outsideless room and a room with Nothing outside it?

More than any other faith Zen has recognized the absurdity of attempting altogether to escape from language. There is Nothing outside language, there is nothing outside language, there is no thing outside language ... yet Zen still obstinately follows nearly all other faiths and philosophies in locating salvation outside language in an effable Beyond. It is clever, yet it continues trying to point us beyond the text, even though it perceives so clearly that there is nothing to point to and no way of pointing to it.

> Buddha, according to a sutra, once said: 'Stop, stop. Do not speak. The ultimate truth is not even to think.
>
> *Ambon's comment*: Where did that so-called teaching come from? How is it that one could not even think it? Suppose someone spoke about it; then what became of it?[1]

An earlier tradition, slightly less refined than Zen, favoured the use of demonstratives like *this* and *that*. They point but don't of themselves say what they are pointing to. Demonstratives have no meaning, only a use. A sentence with a demonstrative in it gets a determinate meaning only in being used on some particular occasion when a speaker employs it according to the custom in an established language-game. Is there then a religious use of demonstratives that succeeds in pointing outside language, without specifying what it is that is pointed to? Alas, no, because no pointing is done until something is being pointed out or to. The preposition is internal to the verb. Otherwise put, demonstratives like 'this' get a meaning only when they are successfully used and something has been indicated or pointed at. Till then, they are hanging fire, waiting to get a meaning. The Buddhist teacher is attempting simultaneously to point to the religious object *and* to say that there's nothing to point to. So he doesn't point at all. He just talks nonsense.

Zen is smart, because it sees this too. It sees that paradox goes all the way down to the very first stirrings of the impulse to jump outside language. No faith has been more acutely conscious of the paradoxicality of its own ambition. So why does it persist in its ambition: why does it go on with an attempt at transcendence that it knows to be paradoxical at its very root? Why indeed does it spend nearly all of its time in pointing out its own absurdity?

An answer that may be unexpected, but is well worth considering, is this: religion in the high civilizations was at the centre of culture. It functioned as a consciousness-raiser and school of intelligence. All major faiths play about with attempts to use language to transcend language, tell parables and other stories whose message is anti-story, teach riddles that open abysses of reflexivity, and generally indulge in various sorts of language-bending exercise in order to show us what language is. Zen simply *is* its own delight in its own paradoxicality, and religion simply is the free play of pure intelligence. If Zen can make you bright enough to understand its stories, then you understand the human condition, so far as it can be understood. And that understanding of why there is nothing to be understood just is religion.

As evidence for this interpretation I offer the Zen stories themselves, which so often delight less in the joys of Emptiness than in the dialectics and the paradoxes of religious thought. Of course Zen refutes itself, but that's the joke and that's the point. Just by using language to express its own ambition to escape from language, Zen is already refuting itself, and knows it. Zen teaches by using riddles (koan), poems (haiku) and stories – and these things implicate it in narrativity, binding it back into the human world even as it tries to escape. Just the flow of a single sentence generates and fills time, makes and destroys, creates a world, arouses the passions, beguiles the night and defers death. So as soon as the Zen teacher frames even a sentence, he pours himself out into everything that he is ostensibly telling us we should renounce. His effort to get out of the world curves back into the world. It is bound to.

And he knows it. I said he was clever. But that means that Zen and every other developed religious and philosophical tradition functions objectively as an education in semiotic naturalism. That is, it returns us at last into the stories and the images. There is only the world of signs. Like every sort of fiction Zen had to posit its own Other, the mundane factual world, in order to tell its own story of escape from it. But in overcoming and refuting its own Other, Zen also refuted itself – and so fell back into, its own delight in its own playfulness. Religion is, philosophy is, the language in which it is conducted. When we try to postulate something real out there beyond the world of signs – God, Nirvana, substance, Matter, the Absolute, reality, or whatever – we do so for the sake of the delicious, exhilarating play of paradoxes that our ambition generates. That play of paradoxes stirs intelligence, enhances life and returns us into the world of signs refreshed and delighted. That is why people have said that God is the desire for God, God is the images of God, and that the quest for God is as if one were to go all around the world and return to one's starting-point.

(b) Keeping going

If religious thought is inherently paradoxical, so that every expedition that sets off in search of transcendence can end only with the inevitable return into immanence, why go on with it? Good question. It deserves a detailed answer, because I am going to be disagreeing with some great figures. I maintain, for example, that when Ludwig Feuerbach had successfully reduced theology to anthropology he should not thereupon have given up theology, as he soon did.[2] He should have continued with it, because the aspiration after transcendence and then the subsequent return into immanence is a dual movement of the spirit that we need to keep on making. We must keep on first projecting God out into objectivity and then, as we realize once again the projected character of all our religious ideas, we have to pull God back once more into humanity. There is here a repeating and almost mythic cycle of objectification and return, dualism and non-dualism. We know we cannot really get out of narrativity, that is, the human world of language and stories and time. Our whole life is lived in and by stories. Stories are all the time projecting forward our future and backwards our past. By our stories we are situated in a time-scale, and by stories we are given our roles to play. Stories evoke our desires and show us how to fulfil them. Stories give us our *place* in life. We live in stories and cannot get out of them. Yet it remains important that we keep up the old illusory attempt to do so. We have to go on telling our queer anti-story stories about how we can escape from the world of stories. When they fail, as they must, our dreams of escape and transcendence will at least have the beneficial side-effect of renewing our understanding of how and why it is that this, here and now – as, for example, this particular chain of signs that you are now scanning – is all there is for us, and all there could be. (And it is good enough anyway, so what are we complaining about?)

Religion on the account I am proposing is pretty much what philosophy is on Wittgenstein's account, a cure for itself, a therapeutic practice. You strive after Heaven in order to learn the wisdom of the return to earth; you try to love something superhuman in order to learn why you must be content to love the human. The true religion is an anti-religion whose practice cures you of religion by fully returning you into the human world. You sought the Holy out beyond the human world, and found yourself forced back into the human world, able now to recognize the holiness of our co-humanity. This holy common world of ours is a communications network, and a world of inter-subjectivity. We are all one body, and it is made of messages flying back and forth. It is the world of signs and time and contingency. It is this world, our world, outsideless as we now see, outsideless in a way that even Zen does not fully grasp. And we go on needing to renew our sense of that outsidelessness, so that we can say yes to our fictionality.

I am saying, then, that the quest for the transcendent is a *felix culpa*, a happy fault, a life-enhancing mistake that we need to keep on making. We feared that the failure of the quest for transcendence might lead to an eternal disappointment. But our philosophic therapy convinced us of outsidelessness and showed us that we had lost nothing, so we were able to transform our yearning for Yonder into love. In philosophy there is a certain sense in which you have to have made the errors of platonism in order to return from the right direction and in the right way into linguistic naturalism or (an alternative name for the same thing) semiotic materialism. I am not saying that linguistic naturalism is dogmatically true, for one should not say that of anything, but I am saying that there is something vital and wise and life-enhancing in the move that Wittgenstein taught us to make, from platonic realism back into language-naturalism. Truth's not in positions, but in moves. First we need to make the mistake of believing in immaterial intelligible things out there, such as meanings, rules, values, thoughts, concepts and the like; and then we must come to see that that belief is paradoxical. It refutes itself, for it cannot escape the words in which it is couched. Why were we trying to attribute extra-linguistic existence to a whole array of spooky little pseudo-objects? Crazy. So we find ourselves returning into ordinary language and usages. As we make the move and give up our error, we get a flash of insight. We see, briefly, that all words are nothing but their own customary usage. There is only a vast, slowly-evolving body of customs. A weird insight, which as I am sure you have already noticed is reflexively paradoxical. For a moment, we had an impossible God's-eye-view of the character of our human life in this world. Hume was more or less correct. All our meanings and truths are but transient customs. Paradox arises when we apply this insight to itself, asking: What is its own status? The resulting antinomy means that the insight is very fleeting and soon lost. It is an insight that we can't have; it is not for us. But it does a valuable religious job. It gives us a momentary, impossible yet necessary glimpse of how things are with us, and this glimpse reconciles us to immanence.[3]

Similarly, in physical cosmology it is a good thing to have gone through the old pre-twentieth-century antinomies of time and space. Are they infinite or not? Does the Universe have a datable beginning or not, is it bounded or not? Paradox seems to arise either way, as Kant and others have argued. Study of these paradoxes is still the best preparation for seeing the point and the intellectual beauty of the modern finite-but-unbounded cosmos.

Thus there is a certain sense in which both semiotic materialism in philosophy, and the theory of the cosmos as finite but unbounded in natural science, can be interpreted as therapeutic doctrines. To understand them, you have to understand the disorders of thought for which they are the remedies. Therapeutic philosophy says, and it is a very tough doctrine, that we should give up 'truth' and instead think in terms of remedial moves, therapeutic procedures that have to be devised from time to time as new disorders manifest themselves.

Now, in religion, I have no new dogma. I am teaching play, I am teaching fictionalism and holy-common religious humanism, and I am saying that the move to these ideas is therapeutic. We come at them on the rebound from the failure of the old quest for transcendence, for reality and for dogmatic truth. The quest, its failure, the rebound and the return into immanence and play have all to be constantly renewed: that is fictionalism. And the return from theism into holy-common religious humanism – that is Incarnation.

In ethical terms, you need to have been jilted by God in order to stir up enough passion for you truly to love your neighbour. You need to have postulated and yearned after an infinite Perfection and ground of all value beyond the world, so that you can return into this world with a sufficient head of steam to be able selflessly to love your fellow human beings. For just in themselves, poor things, they are scarcely any more lovable than you are yourself. The quest for the transcendent winds us up enough to make us able to love the often-not-very-lovable. In the history of ideas we have seen that a humanism that is no longer energized by frustrated religious feeling quickly degrades. Indeed, it becomes anti-humanism. Because of this, religious conservatives can plausibly claim that the death of God is soon followed by the death of man, and religious humanists can *also* plausibly claim that the death of God is redemption for human-kind. The synthesis of the two positions which I am proposing says that the quest for the transcendent must be and will always be reopened, and by its failure must continually renew religious humanism. We have to be religious, and our religiousness has to be frustrated and redirected. Such is the central story of the religious life.

In philosophical terms, it is only by trying to bend language a little bit too far that you can discover its limits. When you have established the limits and accepted them, then you can return the more surefooted into the ordinary and mainline uses of language, and accept them for what they are.

In intellectual terms, we noticed when discussing Zen that, in the past at least, when religion was at its liveliest it was much concerned with raising consciousness and cultivating intellectual play. The tradition of Jesus' teaching in the Synoptic Gospels is full of pleasure in paradoxes, as many oriental readers have commented. Religion enjoys puzzles, problems, flirting with nonsense, multi-layered jokes, infinite vistas of reflections and theological disputation. These things need to be kept going, because they are liberating. That is why the Jews, and also the peoples of Eastern Europe under totalitarian rule, have kept alive a tradition of wry religious and 'metaphysical' humour. The attempt to achieve transcendence is paradoxical, because we are trying to tell a story of a journey altogether out of the world of stories; and the view of the human scene from the fictioned high altitude of transcendence is very comical. So the quest for transcendence is mind-stretching, humorous and revitalizing. When that enhanced consciousness is bounced back to this world we see life for a moment as it is. You get a good view as you are falling to the ground.

At its core, belief in transcendence or in God was belief in the possibility of mastering language from a standpoint outside it. Hence the traditional emphasis upon silence, stillness, concentration and the control of one's thoughts. People were trying as it were to stop the language-generator in our heads which normally pours out language all the time and carries us along with it. Hence too the traditional emphasis on asceticism: you tried to starve your fantasies, reduce the number of roles you were playing in your social relationships, and generally withdraw from time, playacting and history. This was all an attempt to get out of the narrativity that ordinarily rules our lives.

So the religions of transcendence, the ascetical religions and philosophies, were all about the attempt briefly to step out of narrativity into timeless contemplation, and out of language into a standpoint beyond it from which it could be seen and mastered. The result was the creation of consciousness, that unthing, that impossible fiction. Even today consciousness remains a mystery. It is *Geist*, spirit, the God within, a fictioned standpoint outside the chains of signs from which we can look at the chain of signs. Consciousness is religion's creation and religion's legacy to us.

Consciousness needs to be renewed because it too is only a fiction, a paradox and an unthing. It is only transient, not needed, and may easily vanish. The chains of signs can very readily run back and forth without any consciousness, as when you answer automatically, or as people say, without thinking. There doesn't have to be consciousness, and if you value it you will in the long run need religion in order to maintain it.

(c) The redundancy of experience

The chief remaining factor that keeps people loyal to realism and resistant to fictionalism is their belief in experience. Etymologically, an experience is something passed through or undergone. It is a conscious mental occurrence which is thought to be a datum. It is supposed to be uncontaminated – innocent, natural and just given to the mind. It is non-linguistic and yet informative, providing a scrap of direct acquaintance with the world. In short, an experience thus understood is both a psychological event and an experience-of. Being natural and given it can in principle be common, that is, an item of experience may be just the same when it crops up in you as when it crops up in me, and between us we can check that an experience of mine and an experience of yours are indeed just the same. Thus we can assure ourselves that the same item of experience is giving the same bit of information both to you and to me. This makes experience a sufficiently public and common thing for it to be able to do its vital job of tying the common language down to a common world. There is an objective order of things out there, which at least in a number of basic respects appears the same to each of us. Our experiences of it are sufficiently informative, sufficiently common and sufficiently independent of language to be usable to test whether our language is describing the world accurately or not.

If all this is right then natural science must be just organized commonsense. The experimental testing of theories in science is only a more systematic version of a testing of language against experience that we are doing all the time.

However, there is a certain confusion here. Natural science does not test its theories against the world absolutely. It checks its theories only against the vision of the world that is embodied in ordinary language and taken for granted in everyday life. There is indeed much to be said for the view that science is just organized, systematic commonsense; but if so, then science presupposes commonsense and cannot vindicate it. The deep assumptions about the relation of language to reality that are presently in question lie too far back for science to be able to test them. In which case the way the experimental method is used in science to check out theories does not give us a persuasive analogy or illustration for the vindication of realism in philosophy. All it shows us is that so far as metaphysics is concerned science can tell us no more than ordinary language does.

In any case, it is well-known by now that the experimental data obtained by scientists are by no means purely innocent and natural. They have been hand-picked for their bearing on a particular theory, and they are typically presented in the form of measurements. That is, they have been ordered, calibrated, conceptualized and taken into the world of signs. They have had to be processed in this way because scientific theories are already denizens of the world of signs, so that if research data are to be brought to bear upon them then they must be introduced into the same world. Theories are chains of signs, so data have to be signs too. A scientific paper therefore is and has to be an autonomous text wherein theory and data meet on the same level, both having become thoroughly acculturated. The sort of testing of theory against data that goes on in a scientific paper is wholly internal to the text. It does not take us outside textuality.

Science is thus just one more literary subject. Experimental data are then cultural products, and the phrase 'natural science' is somewhat misleading. All science is literary and social. It cannot pretend to be *itself* natural, in the sense of having a privileged and impartial standpoint outside language and culture.

We return now to commonsense empiricism, the belief that all of us have lots of natural and extra-linguistic experiences which we draw upon every day to check that our common language is rightly describing our common world. The vicious circle that arises here must by now be obvious. If experience is to be called upon to tie the common language down to the public world, then it cannot be just private experience; it has to be made common, or publicized. But an experience as such is only a psychological event, so how can it become common property? Answer – it must be taken up into the world of signs. It has to be taken up into language if different people are to be assured that they have the same experience. Thus experience needs first to be correctly described in language, before it can become common enough to serve as a test of how correctly language can describe! The adequacy of the common language to represent an extra-linguistic reality cannot be proved without first being presupposed.

From this circle there is no escape. Objectivity or publicity is produced only within language and culture. We haven't got any independent route to objectivity, prior to language, that we can use to test the objectivity of language's representations.

When I deny the existence of experience, as I do, I mean that there are inconsistencies in the way people call upon experience to justify their realism. In that role experience does no work. It is redundant and it should be fired. Please, rid yourself of experience. It stinks.

I do not deny that all the time swarms of minute flickerings are passing over the face of my sensibility, and that most of them are too vague and ill-formed to be signs. But that is all that need be said. What is not a sign is not significant. Only signs are of any consequence. Only they have meaning, only they can be incorporated into communications, and only they can be published. My experiences are meaningful and objective only insofar as they are already signs. The error of the appeal to experience lay in the supposition that an experience could somehow be meaningful, communicable and cognitively significant without itself already being a sign. We wanted an experience to have all the properties of a member of the world of signs, so that it could get into the world of signs to deliver an important bit of testimony about the sign-signified relationship, while yet we also wanted it to remain a non-member so that it could pass for a genuinely independent witness. We wanted it to be both an innocent outsider and a paid-up member.

The reason for this incoherent demand is simply that there is no standpoint, quite independent of the sign-signified relation, from which that relation can be inspected and reported upon. But many people are strong realists who feel that they must find such a standpoint, in order to be able from it to justify their realism. So they fabricate it. The resulting chimera has some properties of the signified, and some of the sign.

This is not all, for the appeal to experience can sometimes take an even stronger form. Many idioms in our language seem to claim that experience is far more rich, intense, cognitively-informative and generally real than language. Language is only a miserably-inadequate vehicle for conveying it. Real knowledge, like knowing what hunger means or knowing Mary, is a matter of direct personal acquaintance or experience that far transcends mere words.

Such idioms are very prominent in the appeal to religious and similar forms of experience. The philosophy of the Enlightenment was a philosophy of subjectivity. The world was constructed around the reason, the sense-experience and the feeling-responses of the finite human subject. 'Feeling' had to do a lot of work. In some areas of culture claims are made that go beyond simple verification in sense-experience, and these areas became in the eighteenth century somewhat psychologized. They came to be seen as matters of one's feeling-response, one's taste or experience. So we began to hear talk of aesthetic experience, moral experience and in time religious experience.

A certain tendency to internalize religious doctrine and evidences could be traced back to the Reformation and earlier, but in Romanticism religious experience began to take on some of the attributes of God.[4] It was that supremely great and ineffable inward reality to which our religious language refers, but which it is hopelessly inadequate to articulate. A great veneration for religious experience developed, and it is not hard to see why. The old theistic proofs, apologetic arguments and 'external evidences' of the truth of Revelation were getting weaker, so what more natural in the new Age of the Self than that the 'internal evidences' should become correspondingly stronger?[5] If in art we can in the end be guided only by our own aesthetic feeling-response, and if in morality the final arbiter is one's own conscience, then it is not surprising that religion should turn out to be in an analogous position.[6] Besides, a private and internal organ of religious knowledge and touch-stone of religious truth is a most gratifying thing to possess. Negatively it provides you with a last redoubt from which you cannot easily be dislodged, and more positively it is an historical fulfilment of the Protestant principle. It makes religion in the highest degree something inward, spiritual, uncoerced and a matter of private judgment.

These developments stimulated the modern study of mysticism, and also determined the direction it was to take. Mystics were portrayed as being supersensitive souls, like the highly musical. They enjoyed more, and more intense, religious experiences than the rest of us. If our own modest religious experiences are for us a source of religious knowledge, then the far more intense experiences of the mystics ought to be much more informative. It was even suggested that the dogmatic theologies of the past could be replaced by a new Science of Religion built upon the evidence supplied by mystics.

In this way looking to mystics for religious truth became perhaps the most extreme case of the belief in experience. Religious experiences were inner psychological events, they were pure, they were given and they were informative. Above all they were *natural*, that is, they were uncontaminated either by cultural interpretation or by having been coded into mere inadequate words. They were pure pre-linguistic intuitions of the Real. Even to this day many people claim to receive through their own religious experience special God-given private reassurances as to the truth of their own religious beliefs. A queer psychological supernaturalism of what they inwardly *feel* has become their last-ditch defence. They live by the heart, in Wordsworth's phrase.

Yet the scholars who introduced the classic mystical texts to modern readers did not in fact treat them as providing pure natural data. They treated them as books about books; that is, as highly literary texts, standing in a long literary tradition. Thus Evelyn Underhill, introducing *The Cloud of Unknowing* in 1912, points out its close relationship to *Dionise Hid Divinitie*, the English translation of the *Mystical Theology* of the Pseudo-Dionysius. She mentions the four other little tracts in the *Cloud* group, and also the *Benjamin Minor* of Richard of St Victor.[7] Soon the modern reader begins to understand that the scholar of mysticism only ever has texts to deal with. Mysticism is a kind of writing. There is no other form in which it presents itself to be studied. And the only way to explain any text is to show its place in a literary tradition. It is a rewrite of certain earlier texts, recycling traditional metaphors that go back in this case to ancient neo-platonism, to writers like Jerome and Origen, to the Bible, and even sometimes to Plato himself. In short, everything Underhill writes tends to the conclusion that mystical writers are simply *writers*, who have chosen to work in a certain literary tradition. Mysticism is thus returned into its own language, and the concept of religious experience can be declared redundant. It explains nothing outside language. It doesn't deliver anything extra. It does no work. There is only the text, and all attempts to bring in supposedly extra-textual entities, such as the author's personality and intentions or her religious intuitions, are vain because they can contribute nothing to the argument. Nothing extra-textual has any relevance. There *isn't* anything extra-textual.

If along these lines we can talk ourselves into dispensing with experience, then we may see the point of fictionalism. Can you imagine a world in which all subjects are literary traditions, all books are books about books, all talk is a continuation of earlier talk, and all stories are retellings of earlier stories? A world dominated by fictions, built of them; a world in which all your allegiance – religious, moral, political and so on – arise from a free decision to stand in and do your best to keep alive a certain tradition of story-telling and writing?

To imagine such a world is to imagine our world: a languagey, inter-textual fictionalist world, a world of signs, a highly *cultural* world. It was introduced, more than anything else, by German Idealism and by Romanticism. These great movements gave to us an awareness of historical change, and especially of the way language and culture change over time, which has dissolved away the older realistic and authoritarian ways of thinking, and has led us to see human beings as living in a world of cultural signs and stories which they are themselves continually varying and renewing. I have been suggesting that there is a connection between our modern burgeoning of art-forms and fictionality, and the humanitarian ethics of the past two centuries. In strict anti-Western Islam today we can see the links between religious realism, hostility to fiction and the free play of the imagination, and anti-humanism. Conversely, in the West we see the intimate connection between religious fictionalism and religious humanism.

To set up the contrast in such sharply opposed terms is perhaps to make the choice a little easier. Yet we Westerners are curiously ill-at-ease in the world that we ourselves have chosen and made. We have a nostalgia problem. It is a disorder that resembles some forms of neurotic illness: the patient is reluctant to be cured.

(d) Make believe

Often the most obvious things are the hardest to see. It is obvious, or should be so, that culture comes before and determines nature in roughly the way that the net comes before the fish. The mesh of your net and the way you use it determines in advance what sort of fish you are going to find you have caught. Similarly, we don't have any comprehensive and immediate access to nature: we get hold of it only very selectively, by catching it in a net of signs, words and numbers. The theories

and interpretative concepts that prevail in our own day deter-
mine the vision of nature that we currently have. True, some
nets catch more fish than others. But realists are wrong to think
that this shows either that the most effective nets are really
natural objects and weren't made by us at all, or that the best
nets catch everything. Neither inference is valid. What is clear is
that any account of nature that anyone will ever come up with
cannot help but be a cultural product. It has first to be highly
selective, and then it has to be turned into language, coded in
signs. It has to be a chain of cultural symbols. The idea of a
natural order of things out there, prior and quite independent of
language and culture, thus refutes itself even as it is stated. For
when it is stated in words, it is cultural. And as I said, all this is
obvious – yet many or most people still find it very hard to
accept.

When, however, we do get it into our heads that there is no
sense in the idea that our flowing cultural world of signs could
be subordinated to something else outside it and prior to it, and
when we thus free ourselves from the idea of experience as
an independent control, then we begin to see the point of
fictionalism. The world of signs comes first. It is outsideless. It is
endlessly flexible, fertile and proliferating. It produces language,
time and narrativity as the milieu within which we live and
within which, indeed, we are constituted. And so we begin to see
our life as a flowing stream of jostling stories. Even within the
daily experience of just one single individual, the huge volume
and complexity of the narrative material that crops up is hard to
grasp. Each day's events briefly activate such a host of narrative
memories and actforms; each day we play so many different
roles in our varied social relationships with other people; each
day's business finds us taking up and touching upon so many
different stories about our own projects, tasks and daydreams;
and each day we absorb so many different items of narrative
news, art and entertainment.

The temporal movement of life, with its daily flood of
narrative input and role-playing behavioural output, makes it
clear (though, once again, the idea is curiously difficult
to get a hold of) that most or all of our knowledge must be

temporally-extended. It must be like knowing by heart a set of instructions, a text or a melody. It must consist in the capacity to rattle off a whole chain of related behaviour-linked items in the correct temporal sequence. Such knowledge, a narrative sort of knowledge, must include knowledge of plots, of actforms, of the ways people behave, of the way things go, of procedures and so on. And we will need a lot of acquired skill in retrieving the relevant items and joining them together to make up our behaviour-chains. The traditional name for this skill was practical wisdom. The best modern way to get an insight into what it involves is to watch a film director composing a sequence, or a theatre producer in rehearsal finding out what will and won't work on stage. These professionals are trying to put convincing behaviour together, a tough job.

Now the peculiar problem of our modern period, in which the culture has become superabundantly rich, highly differentiated, ever-more reflective, and dominated by the media, is the problem of excess. We have, set before us as options, a far wider range of possible actforms, lifestyles, faiths and philosophies than human beings have ever had to cope with before. What is to be done about this overwhelming flood, which appears to turn so many people into couch potatoes with glazed eyes?

There are various options. *Passive aestheticism*, which for some reason I want to associate with postmodern Japan, says: Let it run. Let the self vanish into the endless dance of appearances. Let the distinction between fantasy and reality dissolve, as in those new simulators that enable you to move about and act within 'virtual reality', a computer-generated artificial world. As things are now, the abundance of available selves, worlds, lifestyles and so forth has become so great that everything is dissolving into a dreamlike flux of images. Including us.

If you find this intolerable, then the second option is *fundamentalism*, which tries to restore the hegemony of one Grand Narrative, and therefore one world, a unified self and a moral order. To do this requires force, it requires censorship, it requires the deliberate exclusion of a great range of options and a great deal of material. Most people, no doubt, therefore still think they can safely dismiss fundamentalism as being cognitively deviant, a little mad and very sectarian. However, this attitude is too complacent. If old-style rationality, reality and morality are indeed disappearing from the mainstream culture we may be losing any standpoint from which we can think of ourselves as entitled to look down upon fundamentalism. It may yet turn the tables upon us; it certainly believes that it will do so.

A third option is *art*. In the face of a cultural avalanche that threatens to overwhelm the self, one way to fight back is to concentrate on trying to produce something of one's own. I try to become an individual through the struggle to express myself in a work that embodies my individuality. One's opus or finished work is a child, a second self, and a consolation because it will live on a while.

This option is popular and tempting. It results from the confluence of two great streams of nineteenth-century thought, one which sought in art a substitute for religion, and another which replaced the old other-worldly salvation with a new quest for self-realization through creative self-expression. Something of the high Romantic view of art is still with us, and I am myself maintaining here both that culture precedes nature and that in an important sense art produces life. The creative imagination sustains the culture by coining new metaphors, inventing new values and fresh nuances of feeling, and by opening up new forms of life.

All that, I allow. But the present issue is somewhat different. We are talking about the problem of the overwhelming and reality-dissolving flood of modern culture. Now it is being suggested that the best way to resist the flood is to add something of one's own to it – and thereby increase it. That is distinctly paradoxical, for the flood is so great and so diverse that it carries away everything with it, including both your contribution and mine. It certainly sweeps away the fantasy that one can hope to cheat death and gain immortality by projecting one's own unique selfhood into a work. To be publicly-intelligible, the work must be composed of general signs – which means that it can never completely express a unique individuality. In any case, you and I are composed of general signs too. We are local privatizations of culture and collections of stories. Our individuality is transient.

All of which shows that although on my own account art is of the highest importance to us, we should not seek in it a way to personal immortality. Because our consciousness of mortality and the only-onceness of life is what *makes* us unique persons, the demand for personal immortality is incoherent.

The fourth option is to attempt by the use of special literary techniques to hoist oneself out of the flux of stories. Our world is a dream, a magical illusion. A special kind of anti-story is needed to wake us up. It works like a slap in the face. I am thinking here of the stories of the Zen masters, of Jesus, of the rabbis and so forth. As we have seen, the wisest of these teachers recognize that there is nowhere to jump out to. Outside the world of language and narrativity there is – tautologically – nothing, because if we could say that there was anything there, we would not be outside language. So religious enlightenment or salvation is an ineffable state of being, a no-thing. Nevertheless, the teachers still believe in it, and go on telling their stories.

We have, however, expressed the fear that this teaching may fail. Zen also refutes itself. It tells stories, too. The world of narrativity and of language is in a very strong sense outsideless, and the preaching of an ineffable Outside is vain. Back comes the answer: 'Zen knows this, too'. Yes, it does – and so it seems to be left saying that one major function of religious teachings is simply to quicken intelligence, to produce delight in metaphysical play, and to keep alive a certain questioning, dancing vitality of spirit. Why? We'll see.

The four options so far discussed remain on the table. There is also a fifth, which learns from the others but is a little dissatisfied with each of them. It begins by acknowledging that our life is only a bundle of stories, mostly half-finished. We are and will for the most part remain a lot of loose ends. We need to accept this and not try to conceal it or escape from it. We cannot now expect to be able to unify our lives under a single master-story, because we do not see how just one story, while still being truly a story, could be uniquely privileged and different in kind from all other stories. Nor can we hope to escape from the transience and narrativity of life into a Nothing and Nowhere outside life. We are not content simply to be borne off by the flood, but nor are we proposing to make of art a substitute for life. No: we will accept that our life is no more than a bundle of stories, mostly half-finished. Our makebelief will be a fictioned belief that, nevertheless, our life still matters, fragmentary and fictitious though it is. We'll have to produce from nowhere, and just by spinning stories, the conviction that our life is worth living.

I am talking then, of a non-cognitive and autonomous sort of faith such as Paul Tillich once summed up in the phrase, 'the courage to be', but it will be made of and sustained by nothing more than storytelling. Because of our need now to find ways of making value out of valuelessness, one of the threads of narrativity running through our life will continue to be our personal variations upon the old story of Christ. His promise of the Kingdom of God to the poor is precisely the sort of promise of revaluation to the devalued that we still need to hear. His fate is a reminder that the human scene will not become less cruel until we begin to dismantle the old machinery of victimization. His life-story can still encourage us to take up the cause of something or other that is currently unpopular and out of favour, and it still embodies the old values of love and recon-ciliation. Reimagined, those values can yet become ours, too.

A second thread of narrativity will be provided by the many stories we tell about our search for a final unity of our life and beyond our life. They will be stories of transcendence, stories of nothingness and stories of outsidelessness. They will in one way and another relate how a yearning for something beyond the world becomes chastened and transformed into acceptance of the world. Loss becomes gain, transience becomes eternal life.

This makebelieve, dogma-less faith will perpetually renew itself by retelling its own stories. What else is there now? And now we can perhaps finally admit that we have after all presented a new master-narrative. It could not be avoided. We found we had lost all the old master-narratives and were now continuously improvising, retelling, embroidering, making it up as we go along. But in relating all this we found that not to have a master-narrative is also still to have one.

Notes

Introduction

1. From Oscar Wilde, *The Happy Prince and Other Tales*, 1888. 'The Devoted Friend' is reprinted in the Penguin volume entitled *Lord Arthur Saville's Crime and Other Stories*, 1954.

1 Words and Time

1. Summarized from G.S. Kirk and J.E. Raven, *The Presocratic Philosophers*, Cambridge University Press 1960, pp. 263ff.

2. Ibid., p. 273.

3. John Baillie, *And the Life Everlasting*, Oxford University Press 1934, cites five previous quotations of the letter – without going back to the original.

4. Kirk and Raven, op.cit., p. 168 (Frr. 170, 171, 169).

5. Because art controls fantasy, it gives us security and the confidence to face even our very worst fears. In this way small children may easily come to love the fearsome witches and ogres of their fairy-tales.

6. Peter Nankarrow gave me this idea by answering my questions about Chinese syntax.

7. Nietzsche, *The Gay Science*, §354 (tr. Walter Kaufman).

8. E.g., II Corinthians 8. 8f., Philippians 2. 1–11.

9. V. Propp, *Morphology of the Folk Tale*, 1928, second edition University of Texas Press 1968.

10. C. Lévi-Strauss, 'The Story of Asdiwal'; in Edmund Leach (ed.), *The Structural Study of Myth and Totemism*, Tavistock Publications 1967, pp. 1–47.

11. My friend and colleague John Harvey, who is an academic as well as a novelist, tells me that he uses the term 'motor-principles' much as I use the term 'actform'.

12. Sara and Stephen Corrin, *The Faber Book of Favourite Fairy Tales*, Faber and Faber 1988, is recommended. It has good texts and some useful notes on sources, but not enough on the *unwritten*, oral, traditions of telling which – as in this case – can be important parts of the story.

13. On this, see the discussion of Lyotard's *Le Differend* in Geoffrey Bennington, *Lyotard: Writing the Event*, Manchester University Press 1988, pp. 106–117.

14. Salman Rushdie, *Is Nothing Sacred?* (The Herbert Read Memorial Lecture), Granta Publications 1990, p. 7.

15. Umberto Eco, *Art and Beauty in the Middle Ages*, Yale University Press 1986, ch. IX is an excellent short account of the mediaeval view of art.

16. There is some affinity between the ideas I am putting forward in this book, and the thought of Simone Weil. See for example Peter Winch, *Simone Weil: 'The Just Balance'*, Cambridge University Press 1989, p. 29: '*only in the context of human action, which is an essentially temporal phenomenon*, is it possible to see anything as systematically interrelated'. Winch is summarizing a theme from Weil's early work. See also David Novitz, *Knowledge, Fiction and Imagination*, Philadelphia: Temple University Press 1987, one of the few works from the analytical tradition on the philosophy of literature.

2 *The Power of Stories*

1. E.g., John McCrone, *The Ape that Spoke*, Macmillan 1990.

2. Hans Frei, *The Eclipse of Biblical Narrative*, Yale University Press 1974, especially ch. 2.

3. Good though slightly old-fashioned account in Richard Wollheim, *Freud*, Collins Fontana 1971, ch. 2. See also the literature provoked by Jacques Derrida's celebrated 1966 lecture and article, 'Freud and the Scene of Writing' (reprinted in *Writing and Difference*, Routledge 1978, no. 7). Although it is very out-of-the-way, I particularly recommend F.P. Cilliers, 'The Brain, the mental apparatus and the text: a post-structural neuropsychology', *S.Afr.J.Philos.* 1990, 9(1).

4. Etienne Bonnot, Abbé de Condillac, *Treatise on Sensations* 1754, tr. Geraldine Carr, Favil Press 1930.

5. G.S. Kirk, *Myth: Its Meaning and Functions in Ancient and other Cultures*, Cambridge University Press 1970, ch. II.

3 *Stories and the Self*

1. See p. 5, above.

2. I refer to the James Strachey translation of *The Interpretation of Dreams*, Allen and Unwin 1954.

3. Ibid., pp. 315f.

4. Ibid., p. 334: these passages are to be found in chapter 6(C): 'The Means of Representation in Dreams'.

5. Translated by Mary M. Innes, Penguin 1955, and often reprinted.

6. Ernst Cassirer, *Language and Myth*, tr. Susanne K. Langer, New York, Dover Publications 1953. The full-scale *Philosophy of Symbolic Forms* (1923–31) is dated now, and has been eclipsed by the work of Freud and Jung and their followers. Yet Cassirer's work retains some value: see

P.A. Schilpp (ed.), *The Philosophy of Ernst Cassirer*, La Salle, Illinois, Open Court 1949.

7. See Romans 2. 28f.; II Corinthians 4. 16. Paul appears to write in a way that conflates two distinctions, the Hebraic distinction between what human eyes see and 'the heart' which God's eyes see, and the old Greek distinction between appearance and reality. For the moralization of the outer-inner distinction, see I Peter 3. 3f., which launches a long tradition of criticizing women for being supposedly more keen on outward adornment than men are. Mary Wollstonecraft, in reply, shrewdly refers to the dress uniforms of military men.

8. See above, p. 14.

9. Erving Goffman, *The Presentation of Self in Everyday Life*, New York, Anchor Books 1959.

10. Sonnet XLIII, borrowing from Ephesians 3. 18.

11. See also my earlier discussions in *The Long-Legged Fly*, SCM Press 1987 and *Creation out of Nothing*, SCM Press 1990.

12. I refer to Bunyan's allegories, and to Law's character sketches in *A Serious Call to a Devout and Holy Life* (1728).

13. *A Treatise of Human Nature* 1, IV, 6: 'Of personal identity'; ed. L.A. Selby-Bigge, Oxford 1888, p. 261.

4 Histories and Myths

1. A.C. Danto, *Analytical Philosophy of History*, Cambridge University Press 1965. See p. 137.

2. Erich Auerbach, *Mimesis*, Princeton University Press 1968, p. 15. I paraphrase and elaborate Auerbach's contrast.

3. On all this, see Jacques Derrida, 'Edmond Jabès and the Question of the Book'; in *Writing and Difference* 1967, Eng.tr. University of Chicago Press 1978.

4. François Wendel, *Calvin*, Collins 1963, has details. But when he emphasizes the appeal to Calvin of the idea of Natural Law, he does not point out how that phrase implies that the real world is something written. A law is a certain sort of written imperative sentence. W.J. Bouwsma, in *John Calvin: A Sixteenth Century Portrait*, Oxford University Press 1987, well brings out the unresolved conflict between two Calvins. One, a literary humanist, knows that Christian theology is textual and narrative – and therefore open to endless retelling and reinterpretation. But the other Calvin is an authoritarian realist, who wants truth to be objectified and fixed for the sake of social control.

5. J.-F. Lyotard, *The Postmodern Condition: A Report on Knowledge*, Eng.tr. Manchester University Press 1984.

6. E. Conze, *Buddhist Scriptures*, Penguin 1959, ch. 2; Paul Marett, *Jainism Explained*, Leicester: Jain Samaj Europe, n.d. (1985). The Jain Temple in Leicester, the first outside India, has a series of stained-glass windows illustrating the life of Mahavira.

7. Nakayama Miki (1798–1887), foundress of Honmichi, is one of several Japanese women who have founded new religions. The official publication, *Japanese Religion*, Tokyo: Kodansha International Ltd 1972, reissued 1981, lists six on p. 97.

8. Compare J.L. Mackie, *Ethics: Inventing Right and Wrong*, Penguin 1977, pp. 30ff.

9. Daphne Hampson, *Theology and Feminism*, Blackwell 1990.

10. E.g., Reinhold Niebuhr, *An Interpretation of Christian Ethics*, SCM Press 1936.

11. V.W. Turner (*The Ritual Process*, Routledge 1969) popularized the use of the term 'liminality' for the rather passive and extra-social state of a person crossing from one realm to another, and he also describes Franciscans and others as people who opt to live in a state of permanent liminality or marginality. Which brings them near my notion of a talismanic or transitional object. My own discussion owes a little to Jung and Winnicott, but much more to children's literature.

5 Theological Stories

1. Critical discussion in G.S. Kirk, *Myth*, Cambridge University Press 1970, pp. 12ff.

2. On all this, see the admirable work of Robert Alter, *The Art of Biblical Narrative*, Allen and Unwin 1981.

3. See the Epistle to the Romans, which became the founding document of (at least Western) Christian theology.

4. On Christian epic, see especially the later writings of T.J.J. Altizer, especially *History as Apocalypse*, Albany, State University of New York 1985; and *Genesis and Apocalypse* 1990. Altizer extends the use of the term epic to include the long narrative poems of Blake, Melville's *Moby Dick*, Joyce's *Ulysses* and *Finnegan's Wake*, etc.

5. Ronald Barthes, 'Introduction to the Structural Analysis of Narratives'; in *Image-Music-Text*, Collins Flamingo 1984, pp. 79–124, esp. pp. 110 ff.

6. S.T. Coleridge, *Confessions of an Enquiring Spirit*, 1853 edn., ed. H.St.J. Hart, A. and C. Black 1956; Matthew Arnold, *Literature and Dogma*, 1873. John Drury (ed.), *Critics of the Bible 1724–1873*, Cambridge University Press 1989, quotes and discusses both of them.

7. Paul Reps, compiler, *Zen Flesh, Zen Bones*, New York, Doubleday Anchor Books n.d., p. 39 (*101 Zen Stories*, no. 35).

8. Ibid., p. 110 (*The Gateless Gate*, no. 25).

9. A very important point. Following Plato, the Christian tradition has maintained that the limits of earthly language and thought are transcended in Heaven. Dante in Paradise converses as-it-were telepathically with Adam. But Zen appears to suggest that the limits of language remain unchanged in the heavenly world.

6 Story Anti-story

1. *Zen Flesh, Zen Bones*, p. 128 (*The Gateless Gate*, no. 49).

2. L.A. Feuerbach, *The Essence of Christianity*, 1841; Van Harvey, 'Ludwig Feuerbach and Karl Marx', in Ninian Smart, John Clayton, Patrick Sherry and Stephen T. Katz (eds), *Nineteenth-Century Religious Thought in the West*, Volume 1, Cambridge University Press 1985: '(Feuerbach's) position is that the development of human consciousness is a function of the development of religion', p. 299.

3. Notice that if meaning and truth are reduced to mere customs, then the insight that that is all they are becomes itself vulnerable. Is *it* mere custom, too? So it seems to me that there is a touch of residual supernaturalism even in Wittgenstein. It is inescapable.

4. The OED points out a Puritan use of 'experience' going back to Owen, Bunyan and others, but is hazy about just when the precise phrase 'religious experience' began to be used. But I take it that something approaching the modern notion began to appear in Schleiermacher's circle, though it may not have become fully-developed before William James.

5. Soame Jenyns, *A View of the Internal Evidence of the Christian Religion*, 1776, shows the shift taking place. Terry Eagleton's *The Ideology of the Aesthetic*, Blackwell 1990, has much to say about why the appeal to feeling and inner experience became so prominent from Shaftesbury onwards.

6. Francis Newman, *The Soul, its Sorrows and its Aspirations*, 1849, makes the parallel explicit. The soul is the organ of religious knowledge, just as the conscience is of moral knowledge.

7. Evelyn Underhill (ed.), *A Book of Contemplation the which is called the Cloud of Unknowing* ..., John M. Watkins 1912, Introduction, pp. 5–31.

Index of Names

Alter, R., 158
Altizer, T.J.J., 158
Aristotle, 79
Arnold, Matthew, 127
Arthur, 102f.
Auerbach, E., 86f., 157
Augustine, 63f.

Baillie, John, 155
Barth, Karl, 63, 121
Barthes, Roland, 118f., 158
Bennington, Geoffrey, 156
Birtwhistle, Harrison, 28
Blake, William, 115, 158
Bouwsma, W.J., 157
Browning, Elizabeth Barrett, 64f.
Buddha 42f., 129, 136
Bunyan, John, 75, 157

Calvin, John, 63f., 122, 157
Carroll, Lewis, 107
Cassiret, Ernst, 56f., 156
Chaucer, Geoffrey, 74
Cilliers, F.P., 156
Clayton, John, 159
Coleridge, Samuel Taylor, 127, 158
Condillac, Abbé de, 156
Conze, E., 157

Corrin, Sarah and Stephen, 155

Dante, 47, 63, 115, 158
Danto, Arthur C., 85, 157
Davies, Peter Maxwell, 78
Derrida, Jacques, 38, 156f.
Descartes, René, 21
Drury, John, 158

Eagleton, Terry, 159
Eco, Umberto, 156
Eliot, T.S., 130

Foucaut, Michel, 76
Frei, Hans, 156
Freud, Sigmund, xi, 14ff., 38, 46f., 53, 156
Feuerbach, L.A., 138, 159

Goethe, J.W., 76
Goffman, Erving, 157
Grimm Brothers, 11, 33

Hampson, Daphne, 102, 158
Hardy, Thomas, 72
Hart, H.St.J., 158
Harvey, John, 155
Harvey, Van, 159
Hegel, G.W.F., xii, 122

Hitchcock, Alfred, 18, 41
Hobbes, Thomas, 17, 75
Hume, D., 75, 140

Innes, Mary M., 156
Irenaeus, 63

James, William, 159
Jenyns, Soame, 159
Jerome, 148
Jesus, 42ff., 97ff., 102ff., 114ff.,
　125, 127, 129, 142, 153
Johnson, B.S., 119
Joyce, James, 23, 115, 158
Jung, C.G., 156, 158

Kant, Immanuel, 1, 7, 21, 48f.,
　75, 140
Katz, Stephen T., 159
Kierkegaard, S., xi, 22, 122
Kirk, G.S., 155f., 158
Kyozan, 132

Langer, Susanne K., 156
Law, William, 75, 157
Leach, Edmund, 155
Lévi-Strauss, Claude, 13, 155
Lewis, C.S., 107
Lyotard, J.-F., 93f., 156f.

McCrone, J., 156
Mackie, J.L., 158
Marett, Paul, 157
Melville, Herman, 158
Miki, N., 158
Milton, John, 115ff.
Molière, J.B.P.de, 75
Muhammad, 43
Mumon, 132

Nankarrow, Peter, 155

Newman, Francis, 157
Niebuhr, Reinhold, 158
Nietzsche, F.W., xi, 11, 155
Novitz, David, 156

Origen, 148
Ovid, 56f.
Owen, John, 159

Parmenides, 3
Paul, 12, 59, 63, 114f., 157
Plato, x, 1, 7, 21, 35, 40, 48f., 75,
　148, 158
Propp, V., 13, 155
Pseudo-Dionysius, 148

Raven, J.E., 155
Rembrandt, 42
Reps, Paul, 158
Richard of St Victor, 148
Rushdie, Salman, 20, 29, 156
Ryle, Gilbert, 38

Scheherazade, 55f., 62f., 67, 80
Schilpp, P.A., 157
Schleiermacher, F.D.E., 159
Schopenhauer, A., 16, 53
Scorsese, Martin, 27
Selby-Bigge, L.A., 157
Sherry, Patrick, 159
Smart, Ninian, 159
Spinoza, B., 75
Strachey, James, 156
Stravinsky, Igor, 24, 29

Tillich, Paul, 154
Turner, Victor, 158

Underhill, Evelyn, 148,
　159
Ursula, 42